# Clued In Paris

## The Concise and Opinionated Guide to the City

Dean Dalton + Andie Easton

*The world is a big place unless you know where to look.*

The Clued In Travel Team

# Paris, France

Ah Paris, decadent city of love, how can we best describe you? You're a city with a pulse, so alive, and glowing with white stone buildings and a flowing blue river. You have pastry shops around every corner and restaurants galore, many featuring exotic cuisines…no wonder your residents are in love with life.

From the historical and geographical center of Île de la Cité (City Island) this ancient capital of the Parisii Gauls has survived and flourished for well over 2000 years. It's a proud city, and that pride is well deserved. Every aspect of fine living is represented, from its wines and chocolate, to its fashion houses, and everything in between. Shopping is almost obligatory. How can a visitor not be tempted by such an array of finery?

Fortunately, a great deal of the past has endured here making Paris one of the most interesting cities in Europe. Its museums and monuments, all steeped in history, are like a treasure trove for the curious to discover. If such things hold no interest for you, no problem; one can easily ignore the old and embrace the modern side of Paris and spend the days exploring the avant-garde *pâtisserie* and specialty shops, the edgy Canal Saint-Martin district, or a just relaxing on boat cruise along the River Seine. At night, the theatres and concert halls vie with the sexy nightclubs for your attention. There is truly something for everyone.

The twenty numbered neighborhoods of today's Paris each have their own personality. While Saint-Germain is quaint and quiet, the area around the Opéra-Paris is grand and frenetic. A lively gay scene can be found in the Marais, and people-watching is *de rigueur* in the Latin Quarter.

We love the Louvre Museum, with its vast collection of paintings, sculptures, and decorative art. There, one can see Marie-Antoinette's personal traveling case complete with hand mirror and teacup, and an enormous solid gold jewelry box belonging to King Louis XIV. We love Paris' churches, large and small, many of which offer live concerts at night. The palaces at Fontainebleau and Versailles beckon us as well; one can almost feel the ghosts of those who have lived there. The latter housed a court as large as 10,000 people in its heyday.

As fabulous as Paris is, its sprawling size can pose a problem if you arrive without a plan and have no clue about which sights are worth the money or not. For the traveler on the move who does not have a month to spend there, this guide will be invaluable Our main chapters are literally titled **Not to be missed**, **Try to fit it in**, and **Skip it unless it's your thing** –so that you can hit the ground running.

Go and find your own Paris, one tailored to your particular likes and interests for this is a city that holds a different experience for each person. And as we clue you in, we hope you'll find wisdom and even some humor in our pages.

-Dean and Andie, and the entire *Clued In* team.

# Clued In Paris

*The gorgeous Hôtel de Ville is actually city hall*

©Alán Duke

# Getting a Clue

Hi there. You're about to explore the most concise city guide you've ever come across. One may ask, "Can a guide book have too much information?" Yes, it can. Not everyone wants to sift through pages and pages of analysis of a city's roadways, population growth, and how a building's bricks were laid.

You won't have that problem here. This guide is as easy to use as it is to follow, and below are some basic tips so that you can start investigating everything this 2300-year-old city has to offer. We'll help you decide what to see based on the amount of time you have in this incredible place. After our recommended sights and some fun excursions, you'll find heartfelt recommendations for restaurants, bistros, pastry shops, and cheese shops. After that are some recommended hotels, followed by some helpful information about transportation, local events, money issues, tipping, telephone clues and basic safety.

Each sight page will provide you with an *at-a-glance* layout of the most necessary details such as the days they are closed, their official website address, and interesting highlights that you should know about. The restaurant pages include information on the ambience and noise level so you can choose the exact vibe you're in the mood for.

As you read on, you'll notice short bullet points labeled *Pro Tip, Historic Highlight, Mealtime Clue*, etc., along with an occasional personal message from us to help give you some perspective. Don't skip over these points; they're rich with insight that will set you apart from other travelers. Here are some good clues to start with...

**For specific updates to this edition** and more things to see and do here, check out the Paris page of our website, **https://cluedintravelbooks.com**.

**Location, location, location.** We believe that the location of your accommodation is paramount. Better to stay in a more humble place in the city center than to stay at a fancy resort that's three miles out of town. Unless you're in the thick of it, you haven't really experienced it. In Paris, we prefer accommodations near the River Seine and not too far east or west from the city center. Being near the Seine means you'll have easier access to both the right bank and the left bank. The southern section of the Marais, the Latin Quarter, and Saint-Germain are all perfect in this regard. If shopping is your thing, consider staying in the area of the Palais Garnier Opera House or the Champs Elysées.

Because of its large size, Paris is a city where the neighborhood of your location really will matter. You don't want to use great gobs of time just getting across town and back again. Note that its numbered neighborhoods are called *arrondissements* because they swirl *around* starting at the very center of town with the number one; the two-digit numbers are definitely further out.

**When to go.** The mid-season, mild weather months are the best for getting the most out of Paris. The crowds are at manageable and you can still get a dinner reservation on relatively short notice. Alternatively, the low-season means you can visit even more sights and enjoy the added benefit of lower hotel and apartment rates (and airfares that are not exorbitant.) The winter months can be quite chilly however, so make sure you bring a coat. As for the summer months, they are definitely not our preference because that's when most people have the time to come here. In August, the city is plagued with hot temperatures, unreasonable crowding, and higher prices. Some restaurants actually close during August due to their staff's own vacation time.

We like September through October, and also mid-March through May. Visiting during the completion of the famed *Tour de France* in late July, as well as during *Bastille Day* (July 14), can be a challenge as both turn central Paris into a huge celebration. This can be good or bad depending on your outlook. These events may also cause hotel rates to increase.

**About US passports...** If you need one, it will take awhile so apply for one immediately. If you already have one, make sure that its expiration date will be *more* than four months from the last day of your upcoming visit to France.

**Paris' tap water is fresh, clean, and safe to drink**, even at the public drinking fountains. (More on this in our chapter *Some Final Clues*)

**Voltage:** Unlike the United States, France has 230 electrical voltage as well as a unique socket and plug style. *Your US plug will not fit into Paris' sockets.* That goes for the charging cable of your dual voltage smart phone too. Since most electronic items are dual voltage, your main worry will be these sockets. For a few dollars online, you can buy a *US to France plug adapter* that will enable your US plug to fit into the local electrical sockets.

**The Paris Museum Pass** gets you discounts on museums and sights throughout the city. If you intend to visit both the royal château at Versailles *and* the Louvre museum, then you'll find this to be an excellent value as both are included and allow you to skip the ticket queue altogether. Check the Paris Museum Pass website before you go to see if it will benefit you: **www.parismuseumpass.fr**

   *Note! There are other companies offering tourist passes using a similar name, but we have not found them to be as great a value. Use the link above to be sure.*

**Map it.** The maps on your smart phone are more accurate and detailed than any we could hope to include here. Use them. And if you don't want to be bothered finding a connection as you walk around, just take screen shots beforehand of the neighborhoods you intend to explore and view them as an expandable photo whenever you want, and with no connection needed.

**Plan your trip using the internet.** We've found that the more you plan ahead, the better your visit will be. This includes reservations for your hotel, rental car, tours, entry tickets to sights, and even your nightly meal.

Without planning and reservations, you will not get into the most delicious restaurants, and the best sights will already be booked up. This can all be accomplished weeks in advance. *Clued In Paris* gives you all the websites you need in order to plan an unforgettable stay in France.

*Parlez-vous français?* You don't speak French? That might be okay. Today's generation is more fluent in English than ever before, probably thanks to the internet. Even so, a few words in French on your part are considered good manners and can help to break the Parisian ice. Be certain to greet everyone with *bonjour* (good day/morning) in the morning hours, and *bonsoir* (good afternoon/evening) from noon to night. They are pronounced *bone-zhurr* and *bone-swah.* You'll find that the rest of the conversation after that will probably be in English. Even so, an occasional *merci* (thank you) and *s'il vous plaît* (please) can't hurt. Pronounced *mare-see* and *see-voo-play.*

**Accessibility for visitors with limited mobility** is fairly easy in Paris. Look for our *Stair Scare* warnings throughout this book, including general accessibility mentions for restaurants, so that we can guide you effortlessly from place to place.

**Fahgettaboutit.** These days, you can forget about bringing large backpacks, oversized handbags, and especially luggage *of any kind* into their museums, palaces, galleries, and theatres. Most websites now list the maximum measurements of items allowed inside any particular venue.

**Christmastime:** Most of Paris' sights and museums are closed from December 24 - 26, and there's no Métro train service on Christmas Day. Most restaurants are shut tight on Christmas as well. If you're planning a holiday visit, you might want to take this into consideration and add a few more days onto your stay.

**Hotel Tax:** In Paris, hotels and apartment rentals will charge a daily visitors' tax of €1 to €5 per person, per night for each person. Five-star hotels may charge even more so be sure to ask if you want to be well-informed about the most current, changing rates. This tax is customarily paid in cash directly to the hotel when you check-out, so be aware.

**Accessibility for visitors with limited mobility** is quite easy in Paris. Look for our *Stair Scare* warnings throughout this book, including general accessibility info for restaurants, so that we can guide you effortlessly from place to place. Most of the city's museums are free for those persons, as well as one companion.

**Pharmacies are very easy to find here.** They all carry a wide range of treatments and products, many of which are homeopathic. Unlike other European countries, they are not always marked with any special symbol or signage but you will definitely see them.

**Paris' nightlife is yours to discover.** While we do make a few suggestions in this book, Paris offers a wide range of entertainments at night, including musical concerts, the opera, ballet, nightclubs and discotheques, as well as the various festivities of the Pigalle and Montmartre neighborhoods after dark. Some things just have no language barrier.

**Tobacco shops are few here, but very handy.** While they definitely sell tobacco, they also sell other things you may need so it's good to be aware of them. Look for the sign with a large **T** on a blue or black background. *Tabac* shops (pronounced like *tobbak*) sell post cards, local bus and metro tickets, candy, snacks, pens, lighters, and tape. Some will even recharge your cell phone for a small fee.

**Regarding your arrival at a Paris airport:** Do not accept the car services of a private citizen, no matter how professional or persuasive they may seem. They will say, "Taxi, taxi, taxi!" to arriving visitors. These people *are not legit nor safe.* Official, metered taxi drivers do not leave their vehicles to drum up business inside the airport. Proceed to the Taxi Line outside and look for the cars with a lit roof sign indicating TAXI PARISIEN waiting their turn for passengers.

*The grounds of Châteaux de Versailles are worth your time*

©Richard Soto

# The Areas of Central Paris

Divided into twenty numbered arrondissement districts, Paris is like a giant escargot. Here it is by the most visited neighborhoods along with distinctive personalities of each:

*Île de la Cité (City Island):* This is the original Paris, where the city was founded. It's the home of some important sights, like Notre Dame Cathedral, Sainte-Chapelle (Holy chapel), and La Conciergerie castle. Next door to it (in the River Seine) is the city's other, smaller island Île Saint-Louis.

*La Coeur (The Heart):* This central heart of Paris includes the first and second arrondissement. You'll find the famous Louvre Museum there, as well as the highest percentage of five-star hotels. There are top designer boutiques, Ladurée macarons, and then farther up are the quirkier boutiques of the area.

*Quartier Latin (Latin Quarter):* This Left Bank neighborhood was named centuries ago for the Latin speaking students who lived there and who attended the many universities of the area. It's the home of both the Sorbonne and the University of Paris. You'll also find old cobblestone streets and distinctive cheese shops as well as the famous Rue Mouffetard pedestrian fresh market.

*Le Marais (Marshlands):* This charming neighborhood along the Right Bank of the Seine was once the favorite of the aristocracy back in the day. Now it's the home of Paris' city hall and those who prefer alternative lifestyles. It's very quaint and boasts some cute pastry shops and a small carousel.

*Saint-Germain (Bishop of Paris, St. Germain):* This lovely area on the Left Bank was the darling of artists, writers, and musicians from 1880 through the 1920's. It's still beautiful today and boasts Paris' oldest church, St-Germain-des-Prés for which the area is named. It's also where you'll find the gorgeous Jardin du Luxembourg garden park.

*Montmartre (Martyr's Mountain):* Montmartre used to be a mere village located on a steep hill overlooking a northern section of Paris. It was where the city's patron saint, Saint Denis was decapitated in 250 AD. Later it was the favorite haunt of artists like Picasso, Renoir, and van Gogh. The view is still impressive especially from its church, the famous Le Sacre Coeur. Today the village is extremely touristy in a very annoying way.

*Pigalle (Plaza of Pigalle):* Since the late 1700's, the neighborhood of Pigalle has been known for its women of the night and its bawdy dance halls which featured such naughty entertainments as the Can Can. The

Moulin Rouge club is still there. Today Pigalle still has the majority of the city's sex shops and theaters. You can find it in the area just below the Montmartre hill.

*Les Halles (The Market Halls):* This very central neighborhood on the Right Bank used to be where Paris had its main "fresh market." After many centuries it was rebuilt and is now partially an underground shopping mall. It also includes the chain stores that run along busy Rue de Rivoli, and is an area well-known for its late-night restaurants.

*Avenue Champs Elysées (Elysian Fields):* Named for the Elysian fields of the ancient gods, this grand tree-lined boulevard on the Right Bank is now the center of activity for large chain stores, the famed Lido show, and the city's Arc de Triomphe. It's also the finish line for the annual Tour de France cycling race.

*L'Opéra (Opera House):* The frenetic but fabulous Right Bank neighborhood surrounding the Palais Garnier Opera House is a definite stand out. The whole of Paris seems to naturally gravitate to it, and the area does enjoy some of the grandest restaurants in town.

*La Tour Eiffel (Eiffel Tower):* This large neighborhood on the Left Bank covers all of the area around the famous Eiffel Tower. This includes the shopping street Rue Cler, the Rodin Museum, the Army museum, the tomb of Napoleon, and of course the tower itself.

*Bastille (Plaza of the Bastille):* Named for the plaza marking the spot of the infamous prison that was destroyed at the start of the French Revolution, this area on the Right Bank is very near the gorgeous Gare de Lyon train station.

*Canal Saint-Martin (St. Martin's canal):* This very hip neighborhood straddles a Right Bank water canal that has been there since Napoleonic times. It was a seedy area until just recently, but now it's where young Parisians live and socialize. It's marked by trendy shops, cafés, and restaurants and has a very unique atmosphere. You can even ride one of the canal boats through the locks down to the River Seine.

### Helpful Clue:

Paris' swirl of numbered districts or arrondissement is world famous, and you can always know the general location of the place you're headed to by its postal code. For example, 75001 indicates arrondissement one, 75008 indicates arrondissement eight; 75016 indicates arrondissement sixteen, and so on. Easy!

# Before You Leave Home
## [A Basic Checklist]

**Make sure your passports are not within four months of expiring during your trip.** A few European countries allow three months, but don't risk it.

**Take a photo with your smart device** (or make a copy to take with you) of your passport's main info page.

**Make sure your airplane seats are confirmed beforehand** if you want to actually sit with your children or travel partners.

**Get €50** *(from a US bank)* before you travel, just to have some on you. Your best exchange rate will come from a Bank ATM here in France.

**Call your debit and credit card companies** before you travel because it never hurts.

**Go online to print out a suggested packing list.** You won't believe all the things you were going to forget, like those plug adaptors!

**Prescription medications should <u>always</u> be packed into your carry-on bag.** This is because "checked" baggage can go missing, if even for a day or two.

**Measure the luggage you plan on checking in.** Its height, width, and depth added together will give you the *linear* measurement; most major carriers allow this to be a maximum of 62". It should also weigh less than fifty pounds to avoid an added fee. A bathroom scale usually works, and airport arrival halls always have a large scale for you to use.

**Pack a few small adhesive bandages just in case.** They take up no space, and having something like this in your toiletries bag can save you precious time should they be needed. Never, ever bring new walking shoes on a trip; break them in well in advance.

**Some airports still forbid full sizes of toiletries in your carry-on.** Pack travel-sized minis of 100 ml. (3.4 oz.) or less of sunscreens, lotions, perfumes, toothpaste and mouthwash. If you purchase something liquid here to take home, it will have to go inside your checked luggage for the flight home. Buying wine? Have it shipped!

# PART 1
## [Not to be Missed]

*Sainte-Chapelle is literally built out of stained glass*

©Richard Soto

# Sainte-Chapelle
## [The 800-year-old glass confection of kings]

It's always fun to visit buildings where back in the day a regular citizen would have never been allowed; that's the appeal. In this one, even royal ministers and courtiers were not allowed. This chapel was built expressly to honor and protect the Holy relic the *Crown of Thorns* (purchased from Constantinople in 1238 AD) and was meant for the prayer and reflection of the King and his family only. The fact that we can be inside this chapel today it a rare treat, especially since is it nothing short of astounding.

On the upper level you'll see stained glass making up the very walls of the building. Detailed and colorful, it's hard to imagine the work that went into creating it. To appreciate it to its fullest, time your visit here on a day when the sun is shining.

Live concerts at night are often offered here and are always a pleasure, though the glass is not half as beautiful against a dark sky.

**www.sainte-chapelle.monuments-nationaux.fr**

**Pre-booked, timed reservations are given priority and can be booked through their website in advance.** Note that on busy days, visitors without a timed ticket may not be granted entry at all.

**Located at 8 Boulevard du Palais**
*-on Île de la Cité*
**75001 Paris**

**Intl. calling: (011) 33 1 53 40 60 80**
Local calling: 01 53 40 60 80

**Open daily**
Closed on Christmas Day, New Year's Day, and May 1

### Safety Clue:

No sharp or blunt instruments (or even water bottles) are allowed inside, which is understandable considering the delicateness of the space.

### Dean says,

"The door on the left near the second level altar was the King's private entrance and connects by passageway to the building adjacent where he had living quarters. He could visit privately at any time and almost no one would know."

### Cultural Tidbit:

This little Gothic chapel has no less than 1,113 stained glass windows!

### No Stair Scare:

Sainte-Chapelle is accessible to those with limited mobility from *Monday through Friday only*. Guests will be escorted via an elevator in an adjacent building that leads to the upper floor of the chapel. There are accessible bathrooms there as well.

*The Palais Garnier Opera House is not just any theatre*

©Richard Soto

# Le Palais Garnier, home of the Opéra-Paris
## [A stunning building, inside and out]

Is it a sight or an experience? We think it's both. If you can get a ticket to a performance (in advance of your trip) then do it. Sometimes the opera will be in season, sometimes the ballet. And the Paris-Opera Ballet is one of the foremost dance companies in the world. If you can't get a ticket, make a point to take the audio enhanced self-guided tour because the interior of this theatre is a *must-see* for anyone visiting Paris. We declare it to be the most beautiful building anywhere. It's certainly no ordinary theatre.

**www.operadeparis.fr**

**Pre-booked, timed reservations are recommended and can be purchased through the website above. They can also be acquired by phone, or on-site at one of the Palais Garnier ticket kiosks or ticket desks.**
*Duration of the self tour with audio guide is around sixty minutes*

**Located at the corner of Rue Scribe & Rue Auber**
*-at the end of the Avenue de l'Opéra*
**75009 Paris**

**Intl. calling: (011) 33 1 71 25 24 23**
Local calling: 01 71 25 24 23

Closed on New Year's Day, May 1, and on days when a matinée performance or rehearsal is scheduled. Call ahead or check their website specifics.

### Cultural Clue:

Novelist Gaston Leroux had the Paris Opera in mind when he wrote *The Phantom of the Opera*. Like in his story, the Palais Garnier has several basements and sub-basements, the lowest of which is submerged in water.

### Dean says,

"The exterior façade of the building is currently covered as it goes through a major restoration until the end of 2024."

### Andie says,

"I never tire of visiting the Palais Garnier and am astounded by its beauty again and again. Don't miss seeing the opulent golden Grand Foyer. Operas and ballets in Paris are also performed at the very modern Opéra Bastille theatre, but I prefer this one. There's just no comparison."

### Mealtime Splurge:

If you're not on a tight budget (or are simply famished and no longer care about money) check out one of the plush restaurants near the opera house. Both are historic and have decent fancy food... The one on the left is **Café de la Paix**, and the one somewhat off to the right is **Le Grand Café Capucines**.

### Stair Scare:

At the present time, this historic theatre cannot accommodate those with limited mobility on the tour. Performances do have special dedicated seating.

*The mighty Louvre Museum was once the royal palace*

©L. Osterhoudt

# Musée de Louvre
## [Important art housed in a former royal palace]

Art, art, and more art. And not just paintings and sculpture; decorative items too, some functional or just extremely rare. They say that if you spent four seconds looking at every item in the Louvre's vast collection it would take you three months to get through it all. The reason we mention this is so you'll stop thinking that you can spend half a day here and see it all. You can't. And if you try you'll probably come down with the malady called *hyperkulturemia* and become dizzy and nauseous. Take it slow, see a few sections that truly interest you, and consider your visit a success. Louvre done.

Okay, okay… we know you want us to mention its highlights. The problem is that they're different for everyone. The most famous works are universally loved for good reason… it's because they're cool. The Mona Lisa by daVinci and the Winged Victory sculpture should definitely not be missed.

We personally love the huge, forty-foot-wide Veronese panting titled *The Wedding at Cana* which was stolen by Napoléon Bonaparte's army from the gorgeous San Giorgio Maggiore church in Venice and was never returned. Evidently, the French admired it so much that at the start of WWII it was unframed, rolled up, and put in the back of a truck which was then driven around France until the war was over. Yes, it did sustain damage from the ordeal.

There's a fascinating new wing dedicated to the personal items of King Louis XVI and Queen Marie-Antoinette that we found to be utterly amazing. But go and make your own Louvre discoveries because they are countless; even the building interior is spectacular.

**www.louvre.fr**

**Pre-booked, timed reservations are highly recommended and can be purchased through the website above.**

Visitors with the pre-paid Paris Museum Pass are also welcome to reserve a time slot.

**Located at 99 Rue de Rivoli**
**75001 Paris**
*-enter near the glass pyramid in the large courtyard*
Métro: Palais-Royal Musée du Louvre (lines 1 and 7)

**Intl. calling: (011) 33 1 40 20 50 50**
Local calling: 01 40 20 50 50
Or alternatively, 01 40 20 53 17

**Closed Tuesdays**
Closed Christmas Day, January 1st, and May 1

*Andie says,*
"I think the Napoléon III Apartments are worth the entire visit to the Louvre."

*Historical Highlight:*

During the French revolution, hundreds of the poorest citizens moved into the Louvre (which was a somewhat abandoned royal palace at the time) and made it their new living quarters. They set bonfires on the floor to keep warm and some people even brought their hogs inside to live there with them. Yes, this place is huge.

*Dean says,*

"Whenever I'm inside the Louvre I find myself looking at the ceilings, doors, doorknobs, etc. It truly was one very fine palace."

*No Stair Scare:*

The Louvre is accessible to those with limited mobility. Find the glass pyramid in the courtyard and then head to the front of the queue; there you'll be assisted into an elevator.

# Musée de l'Orangerie
## [Monet's *Water Lilies* in the Tuileries]

This unobtrusive little art museum at the far end of the Tuileries Gardens will surprise you with its exceptional collection of impressionist and post-impressionist art, not the least of which is the full exhibit of Claude Monet's *Les Nymphéas*. This masterpiece completely encircles the viewer with lovingly painted water lilies and gives you the feeling of being surrounded by nature. (Perhaps we should say *masterpieces*, as it takes up two different round rooms.)

After Monet's work has astounded you, you'll probably seek out the drinking fountain or restrooms which are located on the lower level...when you get down there you'll be astounded again by the completely unexpected Walter-Guillaume Collection. It boasts an incredible array of admired painters so if you're an art lover, or are curious to know more, don't miss this gem of Paris.


**www.musee-orangerie.fr**

**Pre-booked, timed reservations are strongly encouraged to avoid disappointment.**
Visitors with the pre-paid Paris Museum Pass can reserve a time slot inline as well.

**Located in *Jardin des Tuileries* (Tuileries Garden)**
**-near *Place de la Concorde***
**75001 Paris**
Métro: lines 1, 8, and 12, Concorde Station

**Intl. calling: (011) 33 1 44 77 80 07**
**or  (011) 33 1 44 50 43 00**
Local calling: 01 44 77 80 07 or  01 44 50 43 00

**Closed Tuesdays**
Closed on May 1, July 14, and Christmas Day

### Historical Highlight:

This structure was built in 1852 to shelter Napoleon III's citrus trees during the colder months. (They were in moveable large clay pots.) Hence the name *l'orangerie*.

### Great Clue:

Musée de l'Orangerie has a first rate bookstore, with an emphasis on art of course.

### Dean says,

"Monet painted his *Water Lilies* late in his life when he was almost blind."

### No Stair Scare:

This museum is accessible to those with limited mobility. There's a stair-free gravel path in the park that can be used for approach, and then a side door for entry into the building. A diagram is posted on their website.

*Napoléon's tomb is a highlight here*

©L. Osterhoudt

# Musée de l'Armée
## [French army museum & Napoléon's tomb]

The expansive area of the French National military museum and tomb of Napoléon Bonaparte is impressive to say the least, and the collections housed there will fascinate even those who have never considered going to this type of museum before. From ancient weaponry to medieval armor for horses, this is a fantastic place and has wide appeal.

We don't want to give away any secrets so go and see it for yourself. Your visit doesn't have to include the Emperor's tomb but there's some remarkable history to be learned there.

**www.musee-armee.fr**

**Pre-booked, timed reservations are recommended for your convenience and can be purchased through the website above.**

**Located at 129 Rue de Grenelle
75007 Paris**

**Intl. calling: (011) 33 1 44 42 38 77**
Local calling: 01 44 42 38 77

**Open daily**
Closed Christmas Day, New Year's Day, and May 1

*Andie says,*

"This entire complex is included free with the Paris Museum Pass."

### Historical Highlight:

The Hôtel des Invalides was originally built as an army hospital and retirement place for French war veterans.

### Cultural Tidbit:

The museum hosts many orchestral concerts for around €10. Check their online calendar for the most current listings.

### Some Stair Scare:

This complex is accommodating to those with limited mobility *except* for the tomb of Napoléon. Because of this, entry is free for these folks.

### Mealtime Clues:

For a snack, head west to the pedestrian street, *Rue Cler* where you'll find cheese shops, bistros, and our favorite Italian deli, **Davoli**.

# La Conciergerie
## [Castle turned prison on Île de la Cité]

From afar, this building looks exactly like a medieval castle and it just so happens that it is one! In fact, it was one of the first royal palaces in Paris and was fortified back in 1214. The Conciergerie will definitely catch your eye from the right bank of the Seine as it rises up along the edge of Île de la Cité. It has been many things throughout its long history, most famously as a prison for those poor unfortunates awaiting the guillotine during the French revolution.

During most of its time it has been part of a larger complex of connected buildings with the Palais de Justice and Sainte-Chapelle. Much of it is still in use today as government offices. Because of this, visitors are limited to the main entrance hall and one upper level. You'll see the special room where Marie-Antoinette was held for months before she was beheaded, plus several jail cells, royal kitchen, and a few other rooms with historic significance. It rarely has a queue to enter and is worth your time. There's something amazing about being inside the place, and their new, enhanced (and free) virtual reality iPads take visitors here back in time!

**http://conciergerie.monuments-nationaux.fr**

**Pre-booked reservations with timed tickets are encouraged.** Tickets can also be purchased at the entrance.

*Note: A discount is offered if you purchase entry for both the Conciergerie and Sainte-Chapelle on the same online ticket. Win win.*

**Located at 2 Boulevard du Palais, Île de la Cité 75001 Paris**

**Intl. calling: (011) 33 1 53 40 60 80**
Local calling: 01 53 40 60 80

**Open daily**
Closed Christmas, New Years Day, and May 1

### Historical Highlights:

This castle went from being a Royal residence to being the official headquarters of justice because the Kings of France abandoned it at the end of the 14th century in favor of residing in the more comfortable Louvre Palace. A section of the Conciergerie was converted into secure prison cells when it took on this judicial role.

The little chapel with a dedication to M.A. (Marie-Antoinette) was the exact spot where she was held prisoner right before her trial and beheading. The larger room shows a re-creation of the general complex of rooms used to imprison her.

### Super-Savers:

Visitors who can enjoy free admission everyday are: those with valid documentation that they're age seventeen or younger (and are here with a parent), Art History students, and visitors carrying the Paris Museum Pass. *All of the people mentioned should still make a timed reservation.*

*Dean says,*

"The jailers of the French Revolution were savvy businessmen. Those in charge of La Conciergerie would offer the families of its wealthiest prisoners the option of paying a mattress fee (for thousands of francs) so that their loved one would not have to sleep on a hard, filthy floor. Once they received the money they would put forth the order for that prisoner to be guillotined. Then they would arrest a new prisoner and offer *that* family to pay a mattress fee, and so on, and so on. Huge amounts of money came streaming in."

*Andie says,*

"Fans of *Game of Thrones* will love the main entrance hall."

*Stair Scare:*

This historic castle is not able to accommodate those with limited mobility.

*At Musée d'Orsay, a discarded train station was reinvented*

©Alán Duke

# Musée d'Orsay
## [A re-purposed train station with masterpieces]

Imagine the most glorious beaux-arts train station from the turn of the last century, located along the left bank of the Seine, and filled with just enough masterpieces to make it viewable in one visit… that's the d'Orsay.

There's something calming about the place, especially if you're lucky enough to visit during a slow time. From Renoir to Degas, Monet to van Gogh, and Toulouse-Lautrec thrown in for good measure, the collections here are gorgeous. This museum has largest collection of impressionist and post impressionist art in the world. It also boasts furniture and photography, and has several spots in which to dine or grab a snack

**www.musee-orsay.fr**

**Pre-booked, timed reservations made through the website above are recommended to avoid disappointment; they cost a few euros more, however.**
*Visitors with the pre-paid Paris Museum Pass should also book a time slot online.*

**Located at 1 Rue de la Légion d'Honneur**
*-along the left bank of the River Seine*
**75007 Paris**

**Intl. calling: (011) 33 1 40 49 48 14**
Local calling: 01 40 49 48 14

**Closed on Mondays**
Closed Christmas Day and May 1

### Great Clue:

Don't miss the section exhibiting spectacular pastels by artist Toulouse-Lautrec.

### Historical Highlight:

This unusual building was once the *Gare d'Orsay* rail station. It was decommissioned when it could no longer accommodate the newer, longer-length trains.

### Andie says,

"The clock at the far end of the museum is really something to behold. If can get near it you'll be in awe of its immense size."

### Stair Scare:

The museum is accessible to those with limited mobility and offers free entry to them, as well as to one companion. Go to Priority Entrance "C."

# *Les Violons de France*
## ~at La Madeleine church
### [Musical enchantment awaits you]

There's just something about attending a musical concert inside a beautiful Parisian church at night. Even if you would normally never go to such a concert, you'll enjoy this. Any concert in any church in Paris will do, but why not start with the best? Hopefully you'll be fortunate to have your visit coincide with a performance of the incredibly talented *Les Violons de France*, a string ensemble that is among the very best.

Its lead violinist, Frédéric Moreau, will leave you astounded and wanting more. And when this ensemble performs in central Paris it's usually at La Madeleine, a stunning Greek-temple-style church just a few blocks from Place de la Concorde.

Tickets can be purchased in advance with a credit card at the website below, or in cash at the door as long as you get there twenty minutes before the performance time.

Information:
**www.violonsdefrance.fr/en**

Tickets:
**www.ampconcerts.com**

**Located within the church L'église de la Madeleine, at Place de la Madeleine**
*-at the north end of Rue Royale*
**75008 Paris**

**Intl. calling: (011) 49 30 86 87 04 12 60**
Local calling: 86 87 04 12 60

**For performance dates and times, check their website.**

### Get a Clue:

Seating is first come, first served, so don't be late! The front of La Madeleine has better acoustics than the back.

### Cultural Tidbit:

Vivaldi's *Four Seasons* is one of this ensemble's specialties.

### Stair Scare:

This historic church is not currently able to accommodate those with limited mobility.

*Château de Fontainebleau is our new favorite palace*

©Alán Duke

# A Trip to Château de Fontainebleau
## [Napoléonic glory at every turn]

*Half-day excursion*

Perhaps you have already visited the palace at Versailles and long to see a different one… perhaps you simply want to see a former royal palace without thousands of people around you. Consider a side trip to Napoléon's favorite home in the adorable town of Fontainebleau, a very easy forty-minute *Transilien-Ter* commuter train ride from the center of Paris. It's the only Royal/ Imperial château to have been continuously occupied for more than seven-hundred years. Empress Josephine spent time there of course, but so did the earlier French monarchs who built the place. And all have left their mark in one way or another.

A self-guided walk-around should only take about two hours. The affordable entrance fee includes the most important parts of the 1500 room palace as well as its grounds. For a better understanding of its history, treat yourself to the audio guide available in eleven languages. (Tech savvy visitors can download the audio guide right to their smart phone *for free* by visiting the Fontainebleau website below.)

July and August are the two months when you'll need to go early to beat the crowds, or opt for an afternoon arrival when most other visitors are leaving. During these busy months, use your Paris Museum Pass for free entry and ticket-queue skipping.

Alternatively, you can purchase tickets online to save yourself some time and trouble. Note that the first Sunday of each month from September through June is free. We adore this palace and encourage all of our *Clued In* travelers to check it out! It is quite simply magnificent.

**www.chateaudefontainebleau.fr**

**Pre-booked, timed reservations are recommended for your convenience and can be purchased through the website above.**

**Located forty-two minutes south of central Paris (by train)**
*-in the town of Fontainebleau, France*

**Intl. calling: (011) 33 1 60 71 50 70**
Local calling: 01 60 71 50 70

**Closed Tuesdays**
Closed Christmas Day, New Year's Day, and May 1

*Dean says,*

"The interiors here are incredible and include several rooms, including a bedroom, which are unchanged since they were inhabited by Marie-Antoinette. Yes, she had her own apartments here as well as at Versailles."

*Andie says,*

"I do love the palace at Versailles, but the fact that Fontainebleau is so uncrowded most of the time makes a visit here something very intimate and special."

*Travel Tips:*

From Paris Gare de Lyon train station on the right bank, visit the ticket machines and purchase round-trip *Transilien-Ter* commuter train tickets to *Fontainebleau-Avon*. Then ask any of the station assistants who are milling about which track the next Fontainebleau train will be arriving at... they are extremely knowledgeable and speak English. Depending on the day of the week, the train to the château will make only two or three stops, and no change of train is needed. On most days of the week there will be one departing every thirty minutes. Trust us when we say this is a very enjoyable, stress-free journey.

Upon arrival at the Fontainebleau-Avon station, waiting shuttle buses marked with a #1 or a *Château* sign will take you on a fifteen minute ride to the front of the palace grounds. Have euros ready in order to pay the bus driver directly upon boarding, around €3 to €4 per person, each way. The three kilometer distance between the train station and the palace gates is also walkable for most people.

*Great Clue:*

Inside, don't miss the gorgeous two-level Trinity Chapel (one of three chapels within the château) which was built during the reign of Frances I.

*Mealtime Clue:*

There are no snack bars on the palace grounds but there are bathroom facilities as well as a cloakroom for your convenience. In the town you'll find many restaurants, *pâtisserie*, and ice cream shops.

*Historical Highlight:*

The palace and gardens at Fontainebleau *(fawn-ten-blow)* and at Versailles *(vair-sigh)* both enjoy protection and recognition as UNESCO world heritage sites.

*Some Stair Scare:*

The Château is mostly accommodating to those with limited mobility, and entry is free (for one companion as well.) The Chinese room and the Napoleon room cannot accommodate these folks however.

# PART 2
## [Try to Fit it in]

*Marie-Antoinette's bedroom shows her simple taste*

©Richard Soto

# A Trip to Château de Versailles
## [An easy side trip from Paris]

*Half-day excursion*

Of course you can join a guided tour to whisk you to Louis XIV's splendid palace in the nearby town of Versailles, but it's just as easy to get there on your own. We like to take an Uber car there and then rail it back to Paris on the RER train, but *round-trip* by rail is definitely the best bargain. Follow our easy instructions below for an experience you'll not soon forget.

The palace and gardens were the former home of the infamous Queen Marie Antoinette and King Louis XVI (and their court) up until the start of the French revolution in 1797. Let them eat cake? You can get more than cake here... there are several restaurants, cafés, and snack bars for your dining pleasure.

A newly opened wing of Louis XIV rooms (aka the Sun King) is absolutely thrilling and is now included in the independent walk-around, along with the Hall of Mirrors and many other sections of the palace. You can also enter the apartments of the Dauphin (prince), which only recently opened to the public.

The most fun to be had here is in its immense grounds; rent an electric vehicle right behind the palace and see sections that most other visitors won't. Classical music plays from the rooftop of your little cart while you zoom around. Go ahead and park it at the Queen's *Petit Trianon* mansion and then go on foot to see the mind-blowing country hamlet she had built in the 1700's for her own amusement. Walk past the mill and dairy where she and her ladies dressed up like peasants and actually took part in grooming sheep and making cheeses.

**http://en.chateauversailles.fr/homepage**

**Pre-booked, timed reservations are required**
Even visitors with the pre-paid Paris Museum Pass must reserve a time slot.

**Located southwest of central Paris, in the town of Versailles**

**Intl. calling: (011) 33 1 30 83 78 00**
Local calling: 01 30 83 78 00

**Closed Mondays**
Closed Christmas Day, New Year's Day, and May 1

*Pro Tips:*

Ride the city's frequent RER "C" train to get to the palace from central Paris. Disembark at the station stop called *Versailles-Château-Rive Gauche.*

As we said above, we like to take an Uber right to the Château and arrive in style after a stress free, relaxing ride. It will average around €45 depending on which type of car you choose. There are regular bus lines that come here too.

*Pic Click:*

This entire place, inside and out, is one big photo op.

### Historical Highlight:

Those gorgeous twin buildings just across from the front gate of the Château might have you wondering *who lived in them*. Umm, it was the horses. Those are the royal stables and carriage houses. One of them now exhibits all of the Royal carriages and is included with your "Versailles Passport" ticket. Note that it is currently only open on weekend afternoons.

### Dean says,

"I love exploring the grounds by that electric cart; it's fun and beats walking that long distance no matter what the weather. I will never do it any other way again. A driver's license is required."

### Great Clue:

The many water fountains of the palace grounds will be spraying water on Saturdays, Sundays, and holidays from April through October. Check the website for additional special dates and nocturnal shows.

### Super-Savers:

Visitors who can enjoy free admission everyday are those with valid documentation that they're age seventeen or younger. *They must still have a reserved time slot however.*

### Mealtime Clue:

There are many dining and snacking venues at Château de Versailles, some inside and some seasonal ones that are situated outside on the park grounds.

They are all listed on the website. To eat breakfast or lunch at the fancy one called **Ore**, you'd better have a reservation. If you want to bring your own food, the park does offer guests a free picnic area with tables.

### No Stair Scare:

The Château and the grounds are accommodating to those with limited mobility. Upon arrival, use entrance "A" and you will be assisted from there to the appropriate elevator. The palace does offer a way for these visitors to enter free with a companion but call ahead to find out more details.

## By RER train: Central Paris to Château de Versailles

- Take the RER train **Line C** at the Saint Michel/Notre Dame station (heading to the *Versailles Rive Gauche* station) *There are three other Paris stations available to embark as well if you prefer one that is further west of the city center. They are Orsay, Armée, and Eiffel Tower.*

- Inside the RER station, go to the ticket window with *cash* and purchase round trip tickets to Château de Versailles.

- Insert your ticket into the turnstile to enter, and *save it for your exit.* Follow the signs to the platform indicating trains to *Versailles-Château-Rive Gauche.* Once there, a platform sign will be lit with a square yellow light indicating *Versailles-Château-Rive Gauche.*

- When the train arrives, press the button to open the door and board.

- The actual train ride is about thirty-five minutes long. Your station is the last one on this line so *everyone* will be getting off. Do NOT loose your ticket as it may be needed to exit the turnstile at the Versailles station.

- Exit (*sortie*) the station and walk seven minutes following the brown city signs to the palace. Trust us; you'll know it when you see it.

*An EV can be rented to see the fountains*

©Richard Soto

*The unicorn tapestries are inside the Cluny Museum*

©Alán Duke

# Musée National du Moyen Âge
## [Hôtel de Cluny]
### [Museum of the middle ages & ancient Roman baths]

What's with the long title? Well, there's a lot going on here... exquisite tapestries from a time when unicorns roamed the earth, countless medieval items, a basement of Roman baths from 3AD, and all of it inside (and underneath) a mansion held by the abbots of Cluny. All this makes for the best museum in the 5th arrondissement. Located just off Boulevard Saint-Germain, the Middle Ages come to life through its vast collection, and the medieval garden, vaulted ceilings, and unique architecture will cause you to feel as if you've been transported back in time. This entire complex has come out of a long period of renovation and has never been better.

**www.musee-moyenage.fr**

**Pre-booked, timed reservations are recommended for your convenience and can be purchased through the website above.**

**Located at 28 Rue du Sommerard**
**75005 Paris**

**Intl. calling: (011) 33 1 53 73 01 73**
Local calling: 01 53 73 01 73

**Closed on Tuesdays**
Closed on Christmas Day, New Year's Day, and May 1

### Pro Tip:

This national museum is indicated on some maps as simply *Musée de Cluny*

### Great Clue:

One hour guided tours in English are held throughout the year. Check their website for the exact times and days for the month you're visiting.

### Historical Highlight:

This site is two museums in one. The ancient Roman baths cover about a third of the property, with the former gothic mansion of the abbots of Cluny covering the rest. As if this weren't enough reason to visit, the collections held within are impressive by any standard.

### Andie says,

"The recent meticulous restoration of the famous (and mysterious) unicorn tapestries makes the Cluny Museum a *must-see!*"

### Stair Scare:

This historic site is not able to accommodate those with limited mobility.

*The grounds of the Musée Rodin are fascinating*

©L. Osterhoudt

# Musée Rodin
## [A mansion filled with the artist's works]

The gorgeous Hôtel Particular Biron (French lingo for the Biron mansion) was once rented in part to the famous French sculptor Auguste Rodin as a workshop. He bequeathed his works (and his own personal collection of art, photographs, etc.) to the state *if* the Hôtel Biron would agree to become a public museum to house it all. He got his wish. His sculptures are now positioned throughout the lovely grounds as well as inside the mansion.

**www.musee-rodin.fr**

**Pre-booked, timed reservations are recommended for your convenience and can be purchased through the website above.**

**Located at 79 Rue de Varenne**
*-on the Left Bank*
**75007 Paris**

**Intl. calling: (011) 33 1 44 18 61 10**
Local calling:  01 44 18 61 10

**Closed Mondays**
Closed on New Year's Day, May 1, and Christmas Day

*Super-Saver:*

It only costs around €5 to stroll the grounds and sculpture garden which are both open until sundown.

### Historical Highlight:

Rodin's art has been exhibited here to the public since 1919. Before that, the mansion had many other famous tenants including dancer Isadora Duncan, writer Jean Cocteau, and painter Henri Matisse.

### Mealtime Clue:

The museum has an outdoor café in the rear garden offering up sandwiches and salads at reasonable prices, perfect when the weather is fair. The café is usually open the same hours as the museum and can be reached locally by calling 01 45 55 84 39.

### Pro Tip:

If you're really into Rodin then you should visit his home just outside of Paris where additional offerings of his works are exhibited. It's located in the town of Meudon.

### Stair Scare:

This entire venue is accommodating to those with limited mobility. It's free for these visitors as well as one companion. Use the entrance located at 79 Rue de Varenne.

### More Mealtime Clues:

For a snack, head west to the pedestrian street, *Rue Cler* where you'll find cheese shops, bistros, and our favorite Italian deli, **Davoli**.

*Tour boats on the Seine give visitors a different perspective*

©Richard Soto

# Bateaux Parisiens
## [A cruise on the River Seine]

There's nothing like riding the boats which cruise day and night on the beautiful River Seine. While it may seem kitschy, it doesn't feel that way when you're on board and viewing the city from a completely *different* perspective. Knowledgeable commentary means you'll know something about what you are seeing.

There are several different companies running these boats and all have varying price ranges. Our new favorite is Bateaux Parisiens because of their fresher, newer fleet of boats. They offer free audio guides (some right to your smart phone) on most of their one hour cruises. You can also choose a lunch or dinner cruise.

**www.bateauxparisiens.com/en/cruise-tours.html**

**Located at the docks in front of the Eiffel Tower or near Notre Dame cathedral**
*-both are right on the lower part of the quay by the water*
**Central Paris**

**Intl. calling: (011) 33 1 76 64 14 45**
Local calling: 01 76 64 14 45

**Boats depart every half hour**

*Andie says,*

"Such a fun way to see and better appreciate Paris' bridges and waterside monuments."

### Great Clue:

Take a boat ride in the early evening when the museums are at their most crowded. Not only will you get a sunset cruise, you'll have a relaxing rest before your nighttime plans.

### Pro Tip:

We don't recommend booking a ticket in advance on their website unless you really need to be on a certain boat at a certain departure time and are afraid it will be full before you can board. Just buy your ticket in person from the booth at the docks. Easy.

### Some Stair Scare:

Some of their boats are accommodating to those with limited mobility but call ahead to find out which ones along with their departure time.

### Dean says,

"For a fun and unlimited hop-on/hop-off boating experience, check out the new *Batobus* at **www.batobus.com/en/homepage** –they also have tall glass windows and nine different stops. They tend to be slow-moving but it's a fun way to get across town or arrive in style at the Eiffel Tower. Note that the Batobus does not usually run in January and February."

*The* **Musée des art Forains** *literally takes you back in time*

©L. Osterhoudt

# Musée des Arts Forains
## [The sights, sounds and rides of the carnival]

*Forains* translates as fairgrounds, and folks clever enough to snag an online ticket for a tour through this enchanted place will be very happy. It's not easy though because this private museum of one man's antique collection often plays host to movies sets (like *Midnight in Paris*) or special, seasonal events. When it is available, however, the tours do commence.

Delighted visitors will get to experience actual antique rides of many kinds, play competitive games like the "Race of the Waiters," and hear live music from one of the few *calliope* and Hooghuys barrel organs still in existence. It's thrilling in a way that can't be put into words. Children are welcome and everyone will love this very unusual experience. The ninety-minute tour is primarily given in French but some things need no translation. Just go, if you can.

**https://arts-forains.com/en**

*Visits are allowed by guided tour only; a pre-booked online reservation is required.*

**Located at 53 Avenue des Terroirs
75012 Paris**

**Intl. calling: (011) 33 1 43 40 16 22**
*(No reservations taken by telephone)*
Local calling: 01 43 40 16 22

**Private tours are usually given on Wednesdays and Saturdays when available**

*Pro Tip:*

This incredible museum is also known as *Les Pavillons de Bercy* because that was the name of the wine warehouse complex that is used to be.


*Historical Highlight:*

This neighborhood in the 12th arrondissement was once visited by Louis XIV in 1704 to attend mass at one of its churches. When everyone kneeled before him except one man, Louis became furious and had him called over to explain his insolence before the king. The problem was that the man *was* kneeling but did not appear so because he was a giant of sorts. Louis was so amused when the giant stood up that he actually spent a few minutes speaking with him.

The giant explained that he was a wine merchant and that the local wine taxation was having a poor effect on the residents there. Now in a jovial mood, the Sun King declared that the village of Bercy would be exempt from the King's wine tax. It stayed this way for nearly two-hundred years and during this time it became *the* place in Paris to have a wine business. Wine storage buildings, complete with train tracks, popped up everywhere here, and this location is one of them.


*No Stair Scare:*

This venue is able to accommodate those with limited mobility but some specific rides cannot.

*Saint-Germain church boasts a multi-colored interior*

©Alán Duke

# Eglise de Saint-Germain-des-Prés
## [The oldest church in all of Paris]

The famous neighborhood of Saint-Germain is named after a church, the beautiful Abbey of Saint-Germain-des-Prés which is celebrating an incredible 1,000 year anniversary. As the city's oldest church and centerpiece of the area, it holds many masses and hosts a number of events including choral concerts. The extraordinarily colorful interior will probably surprise you.   For history's sake alone it's worth a visit.

**www.eglise-sgp.org/site_v3/wordpress**

**Free to enter**

**Located at 3 Place Saint-Germain des Prés 75006 Paris**

**Intl. calling: (011) 33 1 55 42 81 10**
Local calling: 01 55 42 81 10

**Open daily**
Closed on some special days; check their website for info

*Historical Highlight:*

A church was originally built on this same spot in the 6th century.

*No Stair Scare:*

This historic church is able to accommodate those with limited mobility.

*Tour Clue:*

Visitors are invited for a special tour in English which is usually held on Tuesdays and Thursdays at 3pm. Meet under the organ. (Not available in July for August.)

*Mealtime Clues:*

**Le Bistrot d'Henri** is nearby. (Details in our chapter titled *Feasting*)

*Great Clue:*

If you're interested in old buildings, you might want to take note of the oldest stone house in all of Paris, the supposed former home of alchemist Nicolas Flamel. (Philosopher's Stone, anyone?) It was built in 1407 in the northern part of the Marais district and has quite an enigmatic exterior.

There's currently a fine restaurant installed on the ground level there. It's called **Auberge Nicholas Flamel** and the address is 52 Rue de Montmorency.

*The 19th century home of artist Gustave Moreau is intact*

©Alán Duke

# Musée National Gustave Moreau
## [Unusual art and one magnificent staircase]

The Musée Moreau is a gallery completely dedicated to the artistic works (and some personal effects) of nineteenth-century symbolist painter Gustave Moreau. Located on a residential street in area north of the Opéra-Paris, this former home and workshop of the famous artist is an interesting place to visit, especially on a rainy day.

Some of Moreau's works are unfinished, and his living quarters are so intact with items of everyday life that it causes you to feel like he might enter the room at any moment. The place is rarely crowded and has no audio guides even though it is set up for exploring on your own.

**https://musee-moreau.fr**

**Tickets are required to view the collection and can be purchased on their website**
*Note that online bookings are required if you will be coming here on the first Sunday of the month*

**Located at 14 Rue de la Rochefoucauld
75009 Paris**

**Intl. calling: (011) 33 1 48 74 38 50**
Local calling: 01 48 74 38 50

**Closed Tuesdays**
Closed Christmas Day, New Year's Day, and May 1

*Pro Tip:*

Even if Moreau's paintings are not your thing, plan a quick visit especially if you're in the neighborhood of the 9th arrondissement. It's included for free on the Paris Museum Pass, and the swirly spiral staircase is worth the whole visit.

*Andie says,*

"I can't say I understand this man's artwork, but it's very cool to see his bedroom filled with personal photographs and knick-knacks."

*Dean says,*

"I like his paintings. They are very mysterious and filled with tons of symbolism."

*Super-Savers:*

The museum offers free entry on the first Sunday of every month, and everyday to those under age eighteen with ID.

*Stair Scare:*

This historic building cannot accommodate those with limited mobility.

*The very sight of the Eiffel Tower will stir true romantics*

©Richard Soto

# La Tour Eiffel
## [The iconic Parisian tower]

Monsieur Eiffel built his tower for the 1889 World's Fair which commemorated the one-hundred year anniversary of the French Revolution. It was meant to last around twenty years but is still standing. You can visit its different levels, enjoy the views, kiss, take photos, or even dine in one of its delicious restaurants. The newly renovated first level has a new see-through floor which produces a floating effect, not for the faint of heart.

To proceed on to the tower's upper levels with a booked ticket, go the entrance marked with a green flag. If you don't have an entry ticket and hope to buy one there, go to the entrance marked with a yellow flag.

So, why is the Eiffel Tower in this special chapter? It's because we like it better from afar and now think of it as more of a dining destination. For information on that, read on. And if you find yourself admiring it from afar at night, watch for its spectacular twinkle effect, seen for only five minutes every hour, on the hour until 1am.

**www.toureiffel.paris/en**

**Pre-booked, timed reservations are strongly recommended to avoid disappointment and can be purchased until the day *before* your visit.** *Note that they are almost always sold out way before that!*

There are ticket offices on site too.
**Located at Champ de Mars / 5 Avenue Anatole 75007 Paris**

**Intl. calling: (011) 33 8 92 70 12 39**
Local calling: 08 92 70 12 39

**Open on most days, but check their website calendar for exceptions.**

### Pro Tip:

Because the view is probably the main reason for a visit here, try to go on a clear day. If you opt for the less expensive *stairs* ticket rather than the elevator, make sure you're in good shape.

### Mealtime Clues:

If you'd like a light lunch while on the tower, there are buffet/ snack bars offering various items to purchase. There's also a champagne bar at the very top… *oui, mais bein sûr!*

We highly recommend **Madame Brasserie** on the first level, which is open daily for a *prix fix* breakfast, lunch, or dinner to those with a pre-paid reservation. (Details in our chapter titled *Feasting*.)

### Crime Clue:

At the Eiffel tower, pickpocket gangs work together to take your valuables. But you'll be fine if you keep your wits about you, and keep your wallet out of sight. If unsavory-looking women, often with young children, approach you be on your guard and tell them in a loud voice to get away from you. This usually does the trick.

*Some Stair Scare:*

The first and second levels of the tower can be reached by folks with limited mobility. The third level, which is the highest, cannot. These special visitors are accommodated by elevator lift located at the east pillar where a tower employee will assist. There's an accessible bathroom there as well, as well as on the accessible upper levels.

# Musée Jacquemart-André

## [A breathtaking mansion with art awaits you]

If you're like us then you love visiting a fantastic mansion. This one is exactly that and is filled with art treasures. Its former owners were major European art collectors and their sumptuous home was their showcase. The historic Jacquemart-André mansion-museum is a sight you should experience. Have lunch in their stunning tea room if you have the time.

**www.musee-jacquemart-andre.com/en**

**Entry tickets can be booked in advance to avoid disappointment on busier days.**
There is also a ticket office on site.

**Located at 158 Boulevard Haussmann**
**75008 Paris**

**Intl. calling: (011) 33 1 45 62 11 59**
Local calling: 01 45 62 11 59

**Open daily**
Closed on some major holidays

*No Stair Scare:*

This mansion-museum is accommodating to those with limited mobility.

# PART 3

## [Skip it Unless it's Your Thing]

*The Pompidou contemporary art museum is ugly*

©Richard Soto

# Centre Pompidou
## [Modern art on a grand scale]

Full disclosure: we put the Pompidou museum in this particular chapter because it is not for everyone. Obviously no modern art museum can compete with the level of art on display at the Louvre. We don't love modern art but if you do, this is your temple.

The Pompidou is a large complex, avant-garde in its exterior design, but boasting one of the best and most diverse contemporary collections of art in the world. There's also a very chic restaurant, *Georges*, on the top floor which is a must if your budget can handle it. It certainly has some stunning views over Paris as well as a tasty menu.

**www.centrepompidou.fr**

**Located at Place Georges-Pompidou
(at rue du Renard)**
*-between the Marais and Les Halles districts*
**75004 Paris**

**Intl. calling: (011) 33 1 44 78 12 33**
Local calling: 01 44 78 12 33

**Open daily, except Tuesdays**
Closed on Tuesdays and on May 1st

*Pro Tip:*

If you simply want to go to the top of this building and enjoy the view, ask for the inexpensive *Vu de Paris* ticket.

### Cultural Clues:

Artists, from Munch to Koons to Picasso (and seemingly everyone in between) are represented at the Centre Pompidou. If you crave even more contemporary art, visit the Musée National d'Art Moderne located in Paris' 16th arrondissement.

### No Stair Scare:

This museum is accessible to those with limited mobility.

*Great selection is what Rue Mouffetard is all about*

©Alán Duke

# Rue Mouffetard

## [Quaint shops line a pedestrian area of goodies]

Let's go shopping! Enough of the sights; we want to buy bottles of wine and boxes of chocolates. And there's no better place for this pleasant pastime than on the historic, pedestrian-only street called Rue Mouffetard. You'll see Paris' famous rotisserie chickens dripping their savory juices onto heaps of baby potatoes as everything roasts together. You'll see fresh seafood, adorable shops, and beautiful pastries. There's even an open air farmer's market at one end that has been there forever.

Relax, have lunch, and buy something to take home. At night, the place buzzes with lively restaurants.

**No website**

**Free /Public street**

**Located on the Left Bank**
*-between the Luxembourg Gardens and the Jardin des Plantes*
**75005 Paris**

**Most shops are open Tuesday through Saturday**
*-the Farmer's Market is open in the morning*
Most of the boutiques and stalls are closed Sundays and Mondays

*Pro Tip:*

Online you can find entire historic walks of Rue Mouffetard with fascinating facts about nearly every address you pass by.

### Historical Highlight:

This is one of the oldest streets in Paris, originating from a Roman road. The fountain at #60 is also Roman in origin, and 3,000 pieces of gold were discovered at #53 when it was torn down. Every building here seems to have a history. The street is affectionately referred to by locals as simply *La Mouffe*.

### Cultural Tidbit:

Ernest Hemingway made Rue Mouffetard famous when he called it a *moveable feast*. One can almost feel the ghosts of his literary contemporaries, like F. Scott Fitzgerald and Gertrude Stein, walking over the cobblestones there as they shopped the markets.

### No Stair Scare:

This long pedestrian way is paved and fine for those with limited mobility.

# Montmartre & the Basilica Sacré-Cœur
## [Tourist groups converge on the hilltop]

This village and church atop one of Paris' steepest hills is mentioned in every Paris guidebook ever written. While the church itself is magnificent, we don't love the area around it. It has been systematically ruined by too many kitschy souvenir shops, touristy restaurants, overpriced caricature artists, and overwhelming numbers of tour groups. Couple that with a mélange of seedy characters hanging out... well, that's the scene before you here.

If you like that sort of thing then by all means, go. But if an aggressive man steps forward to knot a "good luck" string on your wrist and then insists upon a €20 note, you had better be ready to shout him away or pay.

(No website for the village)

The basilica is free to enter
 **www.sacre-coeur-montmartre.com**

**Basilica Sacré-Cœur:**
**Located at 35 Rue du Chevalier de la Barre**
**75018 Paris**

**Intl. Calling: (011) 33 1 53 41 89 00**
Local calling: 01 53 41 89 00

**Open every day from 6am to 10:30pm**

### Pro Tip:

This basilica is fantastic and has many things for visitors to enjoy, such as an immense organ, a dome, a crypt, and a fantastic bell tower. There's no elevator for the dome but visitors are welcome to climb the three-hundred steps to the top.

### Andie says,

"Just to get up to the hilltop of Montmartre takes some effort. You could climb the two-hundred-twenty picturesque steps, or use one of your Métro tickets or card to ride the automatic funicular that runs parallel to them. Board it from the base of the hill at Rue Foyatier. It runs from 6 am until 12.45 am daily."

### Dean says,

"We prefer to take an Uber car up to Montmartre's village and then walk down the stairs when leaving, thus avoiding many of the peddlers and con artists."

### Photo Time:

If you're just dying to get some great photos of the quaint-looking village. just go really early in the morning. Note that there are no photographs allowed inside the Sacré-Cœur basilica.

### Some Stair Scare:

Those with limited mobility must enter the basilica at 35 Rue du Chevalier de la Barre. This entrance is open from 9:30am to 5:30pm only! The Montmartre village is accessible at all times.

# Les Catacombes de Paris
## [Walk through Paris' underground cemetery]

If your idea of fun is to enter dark tunnels heaped with the bones of some six-million people, then this is the sight for you. Once inside however, there's no choice but to continue through to the exit which is forty-five to sixty minutes later. Make sure you're up to the task before committing yourself because you'll need to be in good shape.

WARNING: You'll be underground the entire time. It's claustrophobic and chilly (even in summer.) There's no bathroom, and no bag or coat check. There are some eighty spiral staircase steps to climb at the exit. **There are no exit points along the one mile route.**

*Not allowed:*
   Persons with: limited mobility, nervous conditions, in poor health, or expecting
   Animals
   Children under age four

**www.catacombes.paris.fr**

**Pre-booked, timed reservations are required; they can be purchased through the website above.**
Even visitors with the pre-paid Paris Museum Pass must reserve a time slot.

**Located at 1 Avenue du Colonel Henri Rol-Tanguy**
*-within an actual cemetery*
**75014 Paris**

**Intl. calling: (011) 33 1 44 59 58 31**
Local calling: 01 44 59 58 31  **or**  01 43 22 47 63

**Closed Mondays and some major holidays**
*Often closed during part of January and February*


*Super-Saver:*

When they have extra tickets available, their website sells them for around €14 on that same day.


*Dean says,*

"Throughout the tunnels you'll notice old, rusty gates that block entry to sections which are deemed too dangerous for visitors. These gates are never opened."


*Stair Scare:*

The catacombs cannot accommodate those with limited mobility.


*Mealtime Clue:*

Lucky you! The catacombs are within easy walking distance to one of Paris' best bistros, **Joséphine Chez Dumonet**.  Hopefully you have done a bit of planning and secured a reservation for lunch or dinner. (Details in our chapter titled *Feasting*.)

*For an extravagant show, go to the Moulin Rouge*

©Richard Soto

# Le Moulin Rouge
## [Feathers, Showgirls, Champagne, and Cancan]

The newest show at the Moulin Rouge is a visual stunner and even the *entre-acts* between the musical numbers are top notch. This historic cabaret theatre from the late 1800's still thrives and the experience here will not disappoint. It is pricy though. (Feathers must cost a lot these days.) Book a table for drinks or a meal and have a night to remember.

**www.moulinrouge.fr**

**Located at 82 Boulevard de Clichy**
*-in Pigalle, north of the city center*
**Paris 70018**

**Intl. calling:  (011) 33 1 53 09 82 82**
Local calling:  01 53 09 82 82

### Historic Highlight:

This theatre was one of the darlings of the Belle Époque era and later caught the fancy of early 20th century artists like Toulouse-Lautrec.

### Pro Tip:

Online you can choose the date and desired food or drink level but not the actual *table*. One is chosen for you when you arrive so don't come too late.

### No Stair Scare:

This theatre is accommodating to those with limited mobility.

# Musée des Égouts de Paris
## [Down into the sewers we go]

In Victor Hugo's novel *Les Misérables*, Jean Valjean escapes into the Paris sewers. This is nothing like that…

The streets of Paris were first paved with drainage gutters in the year 1200 and their sewers evolved from that. In 1850, engineers extended the sewer system citywide, hence supplying a dedicated water supply to the populace. The Parisian network now has 2,400 kilometers of tunnels for either water or sewage disposal.

In this unique walk-through museum, you'll learn the history and various sewerage techniques from the ancient time period of *Parisiorum Lutetia* (as Paris was called) to the present day. It's perfect if you want to do something really different.

**https://musee-egouts.paris.fr/en**

**Pre-booked, timed reservations are recommended for your convenience and can be purchased through the website above.**

**Located at Pont de l'Alma**
*On the Left Bank near the Alma Bridge*
*-opposite #93 Quai d'Orsay*
**Place de la Résistance**
**75007 Paris**

**Intl. calling: (011) 33 1 53 68 27 81**
Local calling: 01 53 68 27 81

**Closed on Mondays**
Closed on some major holidays

### Great Clue:

Guided group tours are spontaneously arranged when there are enough visitors to warrant it. Otherwise only general entry to the sewers is granted.

### Pro Tip:

This visit takes you inside a section of the actual sewer system which has been converted for this purpose. A large number of models of the fascinating machines used in the sewers are on display in the rooms and corridors.

### Andie says,

There's nothing romantic about this so-called "sewer tour" to me, but it might be fascinating to some people.

### Stair Scare:

This unique museum cannot accommodate those with limited mobility.

*There's a viewing platform atop the Arc de Triomphe*

©Richard Soto

# Les Champs Élysées & Arc de Triomphe
## [Triumphal Arch on the boulevard]

In the middle of a traffic circle on Boulevard Champs Élysées, Napoléon Bonaparte's monumental arch stands proud as it gives tribute to the armies of France. In 1806, the emperor laid the first stone of the arch himself. Today, it's an iconic symbol of Paris and offers visitors who go to the top unexpectedly great views of Paris, especially at night. Underneath it you'll see the city's eternal flame to their unknown soldiers in WWI. The arch does have a elevator but it is reserved for expecting mothers, and anyone with limited mobility or difficulty.

The famous boulevard itself is not worth a special visit since you'll probably find yourself there at some point anyway. It's lined with expensive shops and crowded restaurants and is probably most useful for people-watching.

*Arc de Triomphe information:*

**http://arc-de-triomphe.monuments-nationaux.fr**

**Pre-booked, timed reservations are required for the arch and can be purchased through the website above.**

*Even visitors with the pre-paid Paris Museum Pass must reserve a time slot.*

**Located at Place Charles de Gaulle**
*-located right on the Boulevard Champs Élysées*
**75008 Paris**

**Intl. calling: (011) 33 1 55 37 73 77**
Local calling: 01 55 37 73 77

**Open daily**
Closed on New Year's Day, May 1, July 14, and
Christmas Day
*Weather may also affect openings and times may vary, so call
ahead.*

### Safety Tip:

Don't get killed by trying to run across the traffic
circle... there's a tunnel that goes under the street so
that people can get to the arch safely. Use it.

### Super-Savers:

Visitors who can enjoy free admission everyday are:
those with valid documentation that they're age
eighteen or younger (and are here with a parent), and
visitors with any kind of limiting disability (with valid
documentation) –as well as the person accompanying
them. *They will still need to have a reserved time slot booked
online.*

### No Stair Scare:

The arch can accommodate those with limited
mobility and entrance is free.

# Canal Saint-Martin
## [The cool, edgy side of Paris]

Many visitors to Paris never realize that there's a man-made canal that runs from the right bank of the River Seine, then under the area of the Bastille, only to reappear again in the tenth arrondissement near *Gare de l'Est* train station and continuing well up into the northern section of the 19th arrondissement. That's Canal Saint-Martin. Because it's equipped with locks and hydraulic footbridges, there's actually some boat traffic along it. You can book a two hour boat ride that includes the dark area where it flows underneath the streets but this is not why we mention it...

A neighborhood that hugs its banks (and shares the same name as the canal) is suddenly Paris' trendy area, with interesting shops, bars, nightclubs and casual restaurants. Day and night, young locals come here to hang out or enjoy a coffee at Chez Prune, or sit along the footbridges with their beers and pizza. This section of town is becoming more beautiful (in a quirky way) all the time. There still aren't any top chefs in the area but just wait a year.

**No website**

**Free - public neighborhood**

**Canal-side neighborhood in eastern part of the 10th arrondissement**

*Pro Tip:*

The area around the canal is still rough around the edges so don't go there expecting glamour. Also, watch your step on the old cobblestones.

*Great Clue:*

This is the perfect place to go if you've visited Paris many times and just crave something different.

*No Stair Scare:*

The neighborhood is welcoming to those with limited mobility.

# PART 4
# [Feasting]

## Food Made With Love

*The ubiquitous steak tartar can be found on most menus*

©Alán Duke

Eating well in Paris without spending a king's ransom can be a challenging thing. Don't get us wrong, there are loads of delicious restaurants, bistros, and cafés. The reason we say it can be challenging is that for every great place there are three or four bad ones and we don't want you to end up in one of those. Follow our particular suggestions and you'll have a very memorable dining experience.

But whether you end up in one of our recommended restaurants or not, follow this general guideline: if they offer a "tourist menu" then it's probably not where you'll have the best food. This is truer in Paris than many other cities. Prix fix menus here are the norm and should not be mistaken as a touristy thing.

### Andie says,

"Like most of Europe, the shrimp served to you in some restaurants here will be a goodly size but will likely be presented on the plate complete with their eyes, tail, shell, and spindly leg things. If you're not used to this it can be off-putting. You can request that the chef peel it all off for you –some kitchens will comply and some won't."

### Dining Clue:

Service is slow here; it's a cultural thing. If you must leave by a certain time, just let your waiter know at the start of your meal. The check will never be brought until you ask for it. Use the international sign for *check please,* which of course is an *air-signature* with your thumb and forefinger pressed together... this even works in South Korea.

*Exquisite food with leather-wrapped baguettes (and a view)
at the Eiffel Tower*

©Richard Soto

# Madame Brasserie

The steel and glass which suspends you and your loved ones high above Paris might just take your breath away, but not as much as the food will. Award-winning master chef Thierry Marx has recreated French cuisine into a delicious modern take for today's palette. Located up on the first level of the Eiffel Tower, this is the place to treat yourself, or celebrate a special event. There are usually two different *prix fix* selections to choose from and they do change with the seasons.

*Credit card booking required in advance*

**www.restaurants-toureiffel.com/fr/madame-brasserie. html**

**€€€€-€€€€€**
**Ambience: Classic modern**
**Noise level: Soft**
**Lighting: Natural**

**Credit cards: Yes**
**Accessible: Yes**
**WiFi: Yes**

**Eiffel Tower, 1st level**
Located at Avenue Gustave Eiffel
**75007 Paris**

**Intl. calling:  (011) 33 1 45 55 20 04**
Local calling: 01 45 55 20 04

**Open daily for breakfast, lunch, and dinner**
Closed annually on July 14th

### Great Clue:

You can reach Madame Brasserie by way of a special elevator in the south pillar of the Eiffel Tower.

### Andie says,

"There's nothing like being served exquisite food high in the sky, with the steel beams of the Eiffel Tower out your window and much of Paris at your feet."

### Clothing Clue:

The dress code for this restaurant is smart casual, but definitely dressier in the evening.

*Indulge in exotic  Middle Eastern flavors at Le 404*

©Richard Soto

# Le 404

Don't be fooled by the fact that this is a well-established, family owned Moroccan restaurant. It's one of the sexiest in the city and hard to get into on peak days without a reservation. Exotic décor, hand painted plates, cushions and oriental chandeliers have transformed the high-ceiling'd space without insulting the sixteenth-century structure.

The menu is authentic and delicious, and features *tagines* with olives and preserved lemons, which is served the fluffiest couscous ever. It's a palette change from all those similar offerings at the countless French bistros and brasseries. The semi-open kitchen creates a rustic appeal that's hard to resist.

*Reservations recommended, especially on weekend nights.*

http://404-resto.com/restaurant/paris/404/about

€€-€€€€
Ambience: Exotic, Moroccan
Noise level: Medium
Lighting: Dim, romantic

Credit cards: Yes
Accessible: Call ahead
WiFi: No

Located at 69 Rue des Gravilliers
75003 Paris

Intl. calling: (011) 33 1 42 74 57 81
Local calling: 01 42 74 57 81

**Open daily for lunch or dinner**
*Open Saturdays and Sundays for brunch as well*

### Great Clue:

Families dining with children will be more comfortable during the lunch or brunch services.


### Dean says,

"The wine list and cocktail offerings are vast and keep the late night crowd happy."


### Clothing Clue:

The dress code for this restaurant is smart casual.

*Libertino has made Italian food fun again*

©Richard Soto

# Libertino

For those folks who have heard of the Big Mamma Group, take note; Libertino is one of theirs.

The Italian restaurateurs behind this dining phenomenon may have a strange sense of humor but they have excellent taste in authentic cuisine and have recently taken both Paris and London by storm. Paris now has four of their super-popular, super-creative restaurants and will probably have five or six by the time we type this paragraph. The reason for their incredible success is simple... they give diners a fun, quirky experience through top shelf ingredients, great chefs, friendly service, and interior designs that are usually off the chart. If you love Italian food, definitely book a table online exactly *one month ahead of your chosen date*. You are also welcome to wait in a queue outside.

*Reservations strongly recommended*

**www.bigmammagroup.com/fr/trattorias/libertino**

€€€-€€€€
**Ambience: Garden party quirky**
**Noise level: Medium to loud**
**Lighting: Dim**

**Credit cards: Yes**
**Accessible: Yes**
**WiFi: Yes**

**Located at 44 Rue de Paradis**
**75010 Paris**

**Intl. calling: (011) 33 1 75 85 05 90**
Local calling: 01 75 85 05 90

**Open daily for lunch and dinner**

### Cocktail Clue:

The drinks here are over the top and they also make their own *limoncello* liqueur.

### Clothing Clue:

The dress code for this restaurant is smart casual.

*Be prepared for homemade food at Le Bistrot d' Henri*

©Alán Duke

# Le Bistrot d' Henri

This is the perfect little bistro. With high marks from diners for the French favorites coming out of the kitchen here, the only criticism is that the place is too small. It's the gem of the Saint-Germain neighborhood however, and if you're looking to have that quintessential Parisian lunch or dinner, then look no further. We love the dim lighting and the black and white checkered floor. You'll be fondly remembering their Gratin Dauphinois and reasonable prices long after your visit.

*Reservations recommended, especially for dinner*

**http://bistrotdhenri.fr/en**

**€€-€€€**
**Ambience: Traditional, quaint**
**Noise level: Medium**
**Lighting: Soft, Romantic**

**Credit cards: Yes**
**Accessible: Yes**
**WiFi: No**

**Located at 16 Rue Princesse**
**75006 Paris**

**Intl calling: (011) 33 1 46 33 51 12**
Local calling: 01 46 33 51 12

**Open daily for lunch or dinner**

*Andie says,*

"You may be able to snag a table at lunchtime without a reservation."

*Dean says,*

"I love their zucchini terrine with fresh tomato sauce, listed on the menu as *Terrine de Courgettes et son Coulis de Tomates.* It's so delicious!"

*Clothing Clue:*

The dress code for this restaurant is smart casual.

*Joséphine's Grand Marnier soufflé is worth saving room for!*

© L. Osterhoudt

# Joséphine Chez Dumonet

When you want to experience authentic French flavors in a homey ambience, Joséphine's is the place to go. Located south of the city center,, this scrumptious little place is worth finding. The portions are generous so ordering several courses is unnecessary. They specialize in traditional dishes like duck confit and soufflé. Congratulations to the chef for having recently having won the award for World's Best Boeuf Bourguignon.

*Reservations are a must for dinner, so call way in advance.*

**No website**

**€€-€€€€**
**Ambience: Traditional, quaint**
**Noise level: Medium**
**Lighting: Standard**

**Credit cards: Yes**
**Accessible: Yes**
**WiFi: No**

**Located at 117 Rue du Cherche-Midi**
*-quite south of the Seine* - 75006 Paris

**Intl. calling: (011) 33 1 45 48 52 40**
Local calling: 01 45 48 52 40

**Open Monday through Friday only**

*Clothing Clue:*

The dress code for this restaurant is smart casual.

*Buddha-Bar has been here forever and is still beloved*

© L. Osterhoudt

# Buddha-Bar Paris

The huge, opulent flower-filled, dining room of Buddha-Bar is one the reasons people want to dine here. The forty meter high Buddha statue might be another. It always feels like a party here with many women in sexy dresses and everyone laughing and having a great time. The curated blend of mesmerizing tunes add to the festive atmosphere. We come here for the exceptionally tasty Asian fusion cuisine.

*Reservations strongly recommended in advance*

**www.buddhabar.com**

**€€€€**
**Ambience: Dreamy Asian garden**
**Noise level: Medium / music playing**
**Lighting: Dim**

**Credit cards: Yes**
**WiFi: Yes**
**Accessible: Yes**

**Located at 8 Rue Boissy d'Anglas**
**75008 Paris**

**Intl. calling: (011) 33 1 53 05 90 00**
Local calling: 01 53 05 90 00

**Open nightly until late**

*Clothing Clue:*
The dress code for this restaurant is smart casual to dressy. Some men choose to wear suits.

*Hugo & Co in the Latin Quarter serves up modern classics*

© Alán Duke

# Hugo & Co.

Brainchild of the talented chef Tomy Gousset, Hugo & Co. is the place to dine in the 5th arrondissement. Locals flock here for one of the two nightly dinner seatings to enjoy creative fare that is also approachable. Lunch is also served here and the simple wooden tables let you know this will not be one of these snobby French experiences. A fine wine list completes this relaxed yet gracious food experience.

*Reservations recommended*

**www.tomygousset.com**

**€€-€€€€**
**Ambience: Modern simplistic**
**Noise level: Medium**
**Lighting: Dim**

**Credit cards: Yes**
**Accessible: Yes**
**WiFi: Yes**

**Located at 48 Rue Monge**
*-on the Left Bank*
**75005 Paris**

**Intl. calling: (011) 33 9 53 92 62 77**
Local calling: 09 53 92 62 77

**Open daily for lunch and dinner**

*Clothing Clue:*
The dress code for this restaurant is smart casual.

*At La Rôtisserie, it's like your grand-mere is cooking!*

© *Alán Duke*

# La Rôtisserie d'Argent

Along the quay embankment on the left bank of the River Seine, past those picturesque book stands and merchant tables selling beautiful art prints, you'll find La Rôtisserie. Serving traditional French fare daily, it's not inexpensive but should be considered normal in this part of town.

This will be the best rotisserie chicken you might ever have, served alongside mashed potatoes that are so smooth and buttery that you'll be smacking your lips. For the more adventurous diner, try the half pigeon, which is dark and gamey. We love their six-hour *Coq au Vin* and think it's the best in town.

*Reservations suggested*

https://tourdargent.com/la-rotisserie-dargent

€€-€€€
Ambience: Traditional
Noise level: Medium
Lighting: Standard

Credit cards: Yes
Accessible: Yes
WiFi: Yes

Located at 19 Quai de la Tournelle
*-on the left bank, along the Seine*
75005 Paris

Intl. calling: (011) 33 1 43 54 17 47
Local calling: 01 43 54 17 47

Open daily for lunch or dinner

### Get a Clue:

Save room for the *Île Flotante*, one of their specialty desserts.

### Dean says,

"When you see the red awnings you're almost there. We find the service at La Rôtisserie a bit old fashioned but very gracious."

### Andie says,

"I adore their appetizer plate of herby sautéed mushrooms served with toasty bread. Don't miss it!"

### Clothing Clue:

The dress code for this restaurant is smart casual.

*Serious tapas are found in the heart of the Marais*

©Alán Duke

# Casa San Pablo

You will not be impressed with the look of this small *tapas* joint, inside or out, but don't miss a chance to eat here. The food at Casa San Pablo is served up hot, cheap, fast, and plentiful along with varied beers, wines, and their knock-out homemade sangria. Everything tastes so good that it's difficult for us to make a particular recommendation... the artichokes with crispy ham, the potatoes aioli, and their first-rate Spanish chorizo sausage are probably our favorites.

*Reservations are possible by phone*

**https://casasanpablo.eatbu.com**

**€€**
**Ambience: Madrid-style dive**
**Noise level: Medium**
**Lighting: Dim**

**Credit cards: Yes**
**WiFi: No**
**Accessible: Yes**

**Located at 5 Rue de Sévigné**
**75004 Paris**

**Intl. calling: (011) 33 1 42 74 75 90**
Local calling: 01 42 74 75 90

**Closed on Mondays**
*Lunch service offered on the weekend*
Closed Mondays and on some major holidays

*Andie says,*

"I absolutely insist that you go to Casa San Pablo!"

*Dean says,*

"This wonderful little place is located just steps off the busy Rue de Rivoli, two blocks from the colorful Marais carousel. Cross the street when you get to the Church of St. Paul."

*Clothing Clue:*

The dress code for this restaurant is casual.

*Plump mussels and fries are at Au Pied de Cochon*

©Richard Soto

# Au Pied de Cochon

This is one of the oldest restaurants in Paris and has continuously served patrons since 1947. Its name means *pigs feet* and they still serve them to both the curious and the traditionally minded French folks in the Les Halles district. We're not into that kind of rustic peasant fare but we do come here for their huge steaming pot of plump mussels cooked in a shallot wine broth and presented with some very nice French fries. You'll spot two versions of mussels on the menu but we recommend the *Moules Marinières with maison frites* and not the *Hortence* one that's topped with pork.

Cochon's menu is huge so there's always something for everyone here.

*Reservations strongly recommended for dinnertime*

**www.pieddecochon.com**

**€€-€€€€**
**Ambience: Parisian classic**
**Noise level: Medium**
**Lighting: Natural**

**Credit cards: Yes**
**Accessible: Yes**
**WiFi: Yes**

**Located at 6 Rue Coquillière**
**75001 Paris**

**Intl. calling: (011) 33 1 40 13 77 00**
Local calling: 01 40 13 77 00

**Open basically 24/7**

*Dean says,*

"If you need a place to eat after 10pm, come here because it's one of the few restaurants in Paris that is open late. They finally close around 5am just to clean up and reopen."

*Clothing Clue:*

The dress code for this restaurant is easy-going to smart casual depending on the hour.

*Le Train Bleu is the world's fanciest*
*restaurant in a train station*

©Richard Soto

## Le Train Bleu

There's only one restaurant like this in the world, and that is why we simply had to include it here. It's quintessential "Paris" and its interior has to be seen to be believed. The food is less impressive

While it might just be the fanciest *looking* restaurant you've even been in, don't think that you have to get dressed up. This place was opened with the idea that everyone changing trains or awaiting departure at Gare de Lyon station would be welcome to spend their money here no matter their appearance and they stick to that philosophy to this very day.

The menu is expensive for what you receive which can lead to an overall feeling of disappointment. We think the cuisine here should match the decor and be the most delicious you've ever had in your life. Unfortunately this is not the case. And to make matters worse, the service is lacking, the tablecloths are cheap, and it takes forever to get your check. There, we said it.

*Reservations recommended*

**www.le-train-bleu.com**

**€€€€+**
**Ambience: Baroque elegance**
**Noise level: Soft to medium**
**Lighting: Soft but not dim**

**Credit cards: Yes**
**WiFi: Yes**
**Accessible: Yes**

**Located at Place Louis Armand**
*-inside the train station 'Gare de Lyon'*
**75012 Paris**

**Intl. calling: (011) 33 1 43 43 09 06**
Local calling: 01 43 43 09 06

**Open every day**

### Historical Highlight:

This gorgeous restaurant, named for a famed luxury train that went from Paris to the Côte d'Azur (the blue coast), was built in 1901 and was meant to resemble a palace. And it does.

### Andie says,

"Le Train Bleu was recently refurbished and has never looked better."

### Clothing Clue:

The dress code for this restaurant is casual to dressy and everything in-between.

### No Stair Scare:

Access to this 'upper level' restaurant is by means of an elevator located on the forecourt of the train station, in front of the taxi rank.

*Yes, that's a breakfast burrito in the background*

© Alán Duke

# Breakfast in America

We end our Feasting section with a recommendation for those travelers who have tired of having that requisite croissant and jam for breakfast everyday. For Americans who really need to sink their teeth into something hearty (like eggs maybe?) you need to go to Breakfast in America. It's a New Jersey style diner with real Heinz ketchup and Tabasco on the table. (They have great cheeseburgers too.) There are two locations, one in the Marais and one in the Latin Quarter. Yes, please!

*Reservations recommended*

**https://breakfast-in-america.com**

**€€**
**Ambience: Jersey diner**
**Noise level: Medium**
**Lighting: Soft**

**Credit cards: Yes**
**Accessible: No**
**WiFi: Yes**

*Here's the info for the one on the Left Bank:*

**Located at 17 Rue des Écoles**
**75005 Paris**

**Intl. calling: (011) 33 1 43 54 50 28**
Local calling: 01 43 54 50 28

**Open everyday / Dress code casual**

# PART 5

## [Treats]

**The Perk Report
Pastries
Cheeses
Ice Cream
& Cocktails**

# The Perk Report

Paris has hundreds of pâtisserie (pastry shops) and all of them have pretty good coffee. Order a café crème if want something richer than their standard milk-based version, café au lait. The Café Americain is espresso that's been watered down but will still taste too strong for most Americans. The Italian cappuccino has been wholly embraced here and can now be found everywhere. There aren't many places where coffee is the main attraction, except that green mermaid chain.

The Seattle-based coffee place you frequent at home is suddenly everywhere in Paris so you can definitely seek out your normal coffee faves. In a way, visiting this familiar chain is a cool experience because the pastry and food offerings are completely different from those in the US and are très European, such as Nutella chip cookies. Check out the incredibly beautiful one located near the Paris Opera at 3 Boulevard des Capucines. Hours vary by location.

As for the city's many pastry shops, we focus on the more traditional ones. Of course, that doesn't mean you should dismiss the unique, modern offerings at *Pâtisserie des Réves*, *Des Gâteaux et du Pain*, *Comptoir Le Meurice*, or *Le Comptoir* inside the Ritz Paris Hotel.

# Best Traditional Pastry Shops

## Pâtisserie Stohrer

Since 1730, Pâtisserie Stohrer has excelled at the pastry arts. It is the oldest pastry shop in Paris and has been continuously in business from when its bakers supplied pastry to King Louis XV. In fact, it still sports the original façade and interior décor from 1860. While currently focusing on sweet treats rather than sandwiches, quiches, and savories, you'll never miss them when you sink you teeth into their famous *Babas au Rhum*. It was first created right here! They're offered individually or soaked within a jar for easy take-home. If you like pastry, don't miss this truly historic experience.

**https://stohrer.fr**

**€-€€**
**Credit cards: Yes**
**Accessible: Yes**
**WiFi: No**

**Located at 51 Rue Montorgueil**
**75002 Paris**

**Intl. calling: (011) 33 1 42 33 38 20**
Local calling: 01 42 33 38 20

**Open daily**
Closed on some major holidays

*Get a Clue:*

There is no indoor seating or counters inside this small shop.

*Ignore the mean man behind the counter because the pastries at Bertrand's are great*

©Alán Duke

# Bertrand's Paris - Notre Dame

In the most charming part of the Latin Quarter, near a quaint pedestrian-only street, you'll find the well-established Bertrand's. It's perfect for that quick nosh or cup of coffee or tea and has some tables ready just for that purpose. They also offer top notch homemade pastries, freshly baked breads, sandwiches, and the biggest meringues you've ever seen. *Friendly service?* Not likely, but we recommend it anyway.

**No website**

**€-€€**
**Credit cards: Yes**
**Accessible: Yes**
**WiFi: No**

**Located at 10 Rue Lagrange**
*-on the Left Bank, not far from the Seine*
**75005 Paris**

**Intl. calling:  (011) 33 1 43 25 37 00**
Local calling: 01 43 25 37 00

**Closed Mondays**

*Andie says,*

"Check out their giant elephant ear cookies and rainbow colored meringues. Amazing!"

*Dean says,*

"Their cappuccinos are excellent."

*We love the unique French pastries at A. Lacroix*

©Richard Soto

## A. Lacroix Pâtissier

A stone's throw from the River Seine on the left bank, you'll see a pastry shop that's positioned almost directly across from Notre Dame Cathedral. This is A. Lacroix and the baked goods here are exceptional. Marvel at the suburb artistic creations in their showcase, point to indicate your favorites, and then choose a table in the rear to relax the Parisian way.

**www.alacroixparis.com**

€-€€
**Credit cards: Yes**
**Accessible: Yes**
**WiFi: No**

**Located at 11 Quai de Montebello**
**75005 Paris**

**Intl. calling: (011) 33 1 74 64 14 86**
Local calling: 01 74 64 14 86

**Open daily**

*Andie says,*

"Everything is delicious here but our favorite is the pistachio cream pastry. Enjoy it with a coffee."

*Paul is great for a quick bite between sights*

©L. Osterhoudt

# Paul

Paris' best inexpensive pastry shops have to be the *pâtisserie / boulangerie* chain called Paul. Established in 1889, they are now located all over Paris and have evolved greatly since their humble beginnings in Northern France. At Paul you can grab an overstuffed sandwich of ham and creamy brie, a gorgeous pastry, or even a slice of warm quiche. They always have a counter to sit at for no extra charge, and their coffee is first rate. Now owned by the same company as the ultra famous macaron shop Ladurée, Paul is like the younger brother.

We love the extra friendly service at the Marais location where the Rue de Rivoli becomes Rue Saint-Antoine. Paul makes a great alternative to your (almost always) overpriced and tasteless hotel breakfast offering. Rhubarb tart anyone?

**www.paul.fr**

**€**
**Credit cards: Yes**
**Accessible: Yes**
**WiFi: Yes**

**Located at 89-91 Rue Saint-Antoine**
**75004 Paris**
*Plus many other locations in Paris…check their website*

**Intl. calling:  (011) 33 1 44 59 84 39**
Local calling: 01 44 59 84 39

**Open daily**
Closed on some major holidays

### Get a Clue:

There are locations of this *customer-first* bakery, spreading that French love of pastry, in twenty-nine countries. See our review of its Miami Beach one in our book, *Clued In Miami*.

### Macaron Madness:

If you're intent on trying those gorgeously delicate French macarons, go to the world famous Ladurée located at 16 Rue Royale in the 8th arrondissement. They have other locations in town as well.

# Best Cheese Shops

*Here's a quick cheese clue:*

If you want to go shopping for great cheeses on a Monday you're basically out of luck.

## Fromagerie Laurent Dubois

If you love cheese and want to know more about it, run don't walk to Laurent Dubois. There's a cheese to titillate everyone here. From the stinky ripe to the fresh mild, this place never disappoints. You'll see (and taste) cheese you have never even heard of before and it's a divine experience. The cheeses are set out on a natural wood display which seems very appetizing somehow. The staff there is terrific and will take good care of you.

Centrally located among a row of shops along Boulevard Saint-Germain, you'll see their *Fromager* (cheese-maker) sign set-in among a produce shop, a fish monger shop, a butcher, a salami shop, a wine store, a bakery and a pastry shop. If you happen to be staying in an apartment and feel the urge to cook, this section of street has everything you'll need! Not a bad idea for a picnic along the River Seine either.

**www.fromageslaurentdubois.fr**

€-€€
**Credit cards: Yes**
**Accessible: No**
**WiFi: No**

**Located at 47 Ter Boulevard Saint-Germain**
*-on the left bank*
**75005 Paris**

**Intl. calling: (011) 33 1 43 54 50 93**
Local calling: 01 43 54 50 93

**Closed Mondays and some major holidays**

*Andie says,*

"Many of the cheeses at Laurent Dubois are house-made. Ask which ones."

*Our Cheese Advice:*

If you want to take some cheeses back to the states, be sure to have the shop's staff shrink-wrap them for you. This will enable you to board the plane with them and have them approved by customs/agriculture upon your return home. (This doesn't work for cured meats of *any* kind though, so be aware.)

# Marie-Anne Cantin - Fromagerie

Situated just a smidge off the famous shopping street, *Rue Cler*, this lovely shop in the 7th arrondissement never fails to impress. The assortment of fine cheeses and the extraordinary quality of their product gets high marks in our book. Said to have the best butter in Paris (house-made of course), there can be a line to get in…especially on the weekend. Mix with the locals and give it a try.

**www.cantin.fr**

**€€-€€€**
**Credit cards: Yes**
**Accessible: No**
**WiFi: No**

**Located at 12 Rue du Champ de Mars**
**75007 Paris**

**Intl. calling: (011) 33 1 45 50 43 94**
Local calling: 01 45 50 43 94

**Closed Mondays and some major holidays**

*Pro Tip:*

Any cheese you choose here will be top, top, top. Try a few different ones and expand your cheese horizons. Don't handle the cheeses; allow the staff to assist you.

*Dean says,*

"Marie Cantin herself is often in the shop."

# La Ferme Saint-Aubin - Fromagerie

Located in the heart of charming Île Saint-Louis, the smaller of the two islands in the middle of the River Seine, this tiny shop is packed full of goodies. French cheeses, salami, jams, mustards, and specialty soups abound and can help you put together a killer picnic basket. This is the kind of old-world cheese shop one always imagines being in Paris.

**No website**

**€-€€**
**Credit cards: Yes**
**Accessible: Yes**
**WiFi: No**

**Located at 76 Rue Saint-Louis en l'Île**
*-on Île Saint-Louis island*
**75004 Paris**

**Intl. calling: (011) 33 1 43 54 74 54**
Local calling: 01 43 54 74 54

**Closed Mondays and some major holidays**

*Dean says,*
"The friendly owner does not speak a lot of English but will do his best to tell you which cheeses are his personal favorites if you ask him."

*Our Purchasing Advice (last time):*
Cured meats are not allowed into the U.S.A.

# Best Charcuterie

## Les Epiciers

When you simply must sit down to a platter of top quality cheeses, charcuterie meats and a glass of great wine, no one fills the bill quite like Les Epiciers. Located in the heart of the Marais on the Right Bank, it can be a convenient stop while you are sightseeing. They also excel at classic small plates and really fresh sandwiches. Delicious!

**No website**

**€-€€**
**Credit cards: Yes**
**Accessible: No**
**WiFi: No**

**Located at 33 Rue de Montmorency**
*-on the Right Bank*
**75003 Paris**

**Intl. calling: 33 9 50 50 20 67**
Local calling: 09 50 50 20 67

**Closed Sundays**

# Famous Ice Cream on Île Saint-Louis

## Glacier Berthillon

Since 1954, this shop has been making and selling top quality ice cream. It's now world famous and for good reason; the ingredients and creativity involved is amazing and it's easily the best ice cream in Paris. They even have vegan flavors, made without eggs. You'll definitely find a favorite here. We like the wild strawberry ice cream and the melon sorbet.

**www.berthillon.fr**

**€**
**Credit cards: No**
**Accessible: Yes**
**WiFi: No**

**Located at 29-31 Rue St Louis en l'Île**
*-on Île Saint-Louis island*
**75004 Paris**

**Intl. calling: (011) 33 1 43 54 31 61**
Local calling: 01 43 54 31 61

**Closed on Mondays and Tuesdays, and in August**

*Get a Clue:*

Note that one door is for cones and take-away, and the other door is for table service.

*Dean says,*

"Don't miss the *Griottines Ice Bomb* when they have it."

# Late Night Cocktails

## Le Hibou (The Owl)

For a late night evening with some of the best mixology we've found in Paris, you just can't beat Le Hibou. Food is served as well but we go there for the cocktails. Snag one of the outdoor tables and take in the street scene. The service is not fast so don't expect it. Just sip your Pear Bellini and relax... you're in Paris.

**http://lehibouparis.fr**

**€€-€€€**
**Credit cards: Yes**
**Accessible: Yes**
**WiFi: Yes**
**Outdoor seating: Yes**

**Located at 16 Carrefour de l'Odéon**
*-in the eastern part of Saint-Germain*
**Right Bank - 75006 Paris**

**Intl. calling: (011) 33 1 43 54 96 91**
Local calling: 01 43 54 96 91

**Open daily from morning to late night**

# PART 6
## [Accommodations]

## Hotels to Set the Mood

Where you stay will set the mood for your entire visit, even if you don't end up spending much time there. Just leaving from, or returning to a beautiful hotel gives the traveler an indescribable feeling. We recommend first-time visitors to Paris stay in the city center near the River Seine, in a neighborhood that really appeals to them.

Walk in Tchaikovsky's footsteps at the Hôtel Meurice, or rub elbows with celebrities at the glamorous Hôtel Ritz or Hôtel Park Hyatt Paris. But for those travelers who are more *budget-conscience*, consider a smaller boutique hotel like the Hotel Duo. Some hotels will raise their prices in the summer or during major festival days so consider the calendar when choosing your time to visit. (Details in the chapter titled *Some Final Clues*)

### Hotels vs. online apartment rentals:

If you don't really need a lot of services then consider staying in a private apartment; Airbnb.com is quite reliable here. While the popularity of renting short-stay apartments continues to grow, remember that hotels offer *services* and that's part of what you're paying for.

A hotel might suit your family better than an apartment or vice-versa. The trick is to consider what kind of vacation experience you're seeking here. If you don't need help with the language, don't care about a complimentary breakfast or concierge services, medical attention, or access to a room safe, and are not planning on having a workout or massage then you may not *need* a hotel.

We know that an independent stay in a private home has its charms – just be smart about what you're giving up; if it suits you, terrific. (But it'll never compare to the experience of a truly great hotel.)

### *Pro Tip:*

The star ratings of hotels are *not* generated by a consensus of *people's opinions*. They are actually a strict industry rating, based on a particular hotel's guest services and capabilities. For instance, two very similar hotels can be rated 3 stars or 4 stars depending if one has a restaurant. This system is meant to help you choose a hotel with the level of service and amenities you desire.

### *Some Stair Scare:*

Most of Paris' hotels are accessible for those with limited mobility but we will also indicate it in our listings.

## Hôtel d'Orsay (4 stars)

As the name implies, this lovely hotel is just steps away from the famous and fabulous d'Orsay Museum. Housed in two eighteenth-century buildings, it has been very well cared for. It's old, yet feels new...like you've gone back in time. The location, always an important factor for us, is very central to many of the top museums and designer boutiques. We think it the perfect choice for those visiting Paris for the first time. The service there is consistently friendly and professional.

- ✓ Left Bank, centrally located to the rest of Paris
- ✓ Just off the River Seine
- ✓ Bar lounge
- ✓ Patio area
- ✓ Forty-one rooms
  Not accessible

**www.paris-hotel-orsay.com/en**

**€€-€€€**

**Located at 93 Rue de Lille**
*-Near the Musée d'Orsay, 7th arrondissement*
**On the left bank**

**Intl. calling: (011) 33 1 47 05 85 54**
Local calling: 01 47 05 85 54

*Email contact available directly through their website*

# Hôtel Le Relais Madeleine  (3 Stars)

This adorable boutique hotel is perfectly situated for those attending the ballet or opera at the famed Palais Garnier. Well-priced for its comfortable arrangement and very helpful staff, it may be one of Paris' best-kept secrets. The rooms are not large however, and neither is the elevator but there's a staircase you can use instead. Best part: if you need help or advice with anything regarding Paris, the English-speaking staff will assist you in every way they can.

- ✓ Right Bank, centrally located to the rest of Paris
- ✓ In the heart of the Opéra/Madeleine shopping and theatre area
- ✓ Newly renovated rooms
- ✓ Twenty-three rooms
- ✓ Some accessibility

**www.hotel-relais-madeleine.com/fr/hotel-paris-9eme**

*€€-€€€*

**Located at 11 Rue Godot de Mauroy**
*near the Palais Garnier, in the 9th arrondissement*
**On the right bank**

**Intl. calling: (011) 33 1 47 42 22 40**
Local calling: 01 47 42 22 40

**Email:** contact@relaismadeleine.fr

*Hotel Duo offers comfortable rooms at a fair price*

©Alan Duke

## Hôtel Duo  (3 Stars)

When your taste level (and desire for a perfect location) is at odds with your bank account, you need to stay at Hotel Duo. This humble, well-priced hotel seems to set a high standard for itself and tries really hard to deliver. Even the mattresses feel divine. You might start to believe that you're staying at a more deluxe property. Even the bathrooms, most featuring a large bathtub *and* shower, seem luxurious. Check out the great amenities below and watch for incredible last minute deals.

- ✓ Right Bank, centrally located to the rest of Paris
- ✓ Cocktail bar
- ✓ Pillow menu
- ✓ Fitness center
- ✓ Fifty-eight rooms
  Not accessible

**www.duo-paris.com**

€-€€€

**Located at 11 Rue du Temple**
*in the Marais district, 4th arrondissement*
**On the right bank**

**Intl. calling: (011) 33 1 42 72 72 22**
Local calling: 01 42 72 72 22

**Email:** contact@duoparis.com

## Hôtel d'Orsay (4 stars)

As the name implies, this lovely hotel is just steps away from the famous and fabulous d'Orsay Museum. Housed in two eighteenth-century buildings, it has been very well cared for. It's old, yet feels new...like you've gone back in time. The location, always an important factor for us, is very central to many of the top museums and designer boutiques. We think it the perfect choice for those visiting Paris for the first time. The service there is consistently friendly and professional.

- ✓ Left Bank, centrally located to the rest of Paris
- ✓ Just off the River Seine
- ✓ Bar lounge
- ✓ Patio area
- ✓ Forty-one rooms
  Not accessible

**www.paris-hotel-orsay.com/en**

**€€-€€€**

**Located at 93 Rue de Lille**
*-Near the Musée d'Orsay, 7th arrondissement*
**On the left bank**

**Intl. calling: (011) 33 1 47 05 85 54**
Local calling: 01 47 05 85 54

*Email contact available directly through their website*

## Palace Park Hyatt Paris -Vendôme (5 Stars)

If your taste runs to the more modern and ultra chic and you have a healthy budget with which to spoil yourself, then this is your place. Situated just north of the famous Place Vendôme, this elegant hotel is close to the best shopping Paris has to offer. It's only a short stroll to the River Seine, the Louvre Museum, and the Garnier Opera House. Its wonderful restaurants, cocktail bar, and spa services will make you feel like you have gone to heaven.

- ✓ Right Bank, centrally located to the rest of Paris
- ✓ Five restaurants
- ✓ Award winning cocktail bar
- ✓ Marble baths
- ✓ Room Service
- ✓ Spa Services
- ✓ Hair and nail salon
- ✓ Accessible
- ✓ One-hundred fifty-three rooms

**https://parisvendome.park.hyatt.com/en/hotel/home. html**

**€€€€-€€€€€**

**Located at 5 Rue de la Paix**
*near the other fancy hotels, in the 2nd arrondissement*
**On the right bank**

**Intl. calling: (011) 33 1 58 71 12 34**
Local calling: 01 58 71 12 34

**Email:** paris.vendome@hyatt.com

# Hôtel Signature Saint-Germain (3 stars)

This fun hotel sits on a quiet street right in the heart of the Saint-Germain area. It's near many of the artistic boutiques and cafés of the neighborhood, and is only a short stroll away from the famous Boulevard Saint-Germain. Newly renovated in a quirky style, this place will put you in a good mood the minute you walk in. The prices are mid-range, perfect for visitors who want a special experience for a reasonable cost.

- ✓ Left Bank, centrally located to the rest of Paris
- ✓ Just off the Boulevard Saint-Germain
- ✓ Comfortable rooms with a fun, distinctive style
- ✓ Accessible
- ✓ Twenty-six rooms

**www.signature-saintgermain.com**

€€€

**Located at 5 Rue Chomel**
*in the Saint-Germain district, 7th arrondissement*
**On the left bank**

**Intl. calling: (011) 33 1 45 48 35 53**
Local calling: 01 45 48 35 53

**Email:** info@signature-saintgermain.com

# Hôtel Turenne Le Marais (3 Stars)

The Turenne Le Marais is not fancy, but neither are its prices. It has been recently renovated however, and while the rooms are small (like most in Europe), the bathrooms are quite large. Shuttered windows are easily opened for fresh air or for a view of the Marais area. Nearby is the beautiful *Place de Vosges* and the home of Victor Hugo. The surrounding neighborhood is very safe and has many restaurants, some of which are open all night long. It's also near several wonderful pastry shops and the Métro stop at Saint-Paul.

- ✓ Right Bank, centrally located to the rest of Paris
- ✓ In the heart of the Marais, easy walking distance to Île de la Cité
- ✓ Comfortable rooms, newly renovated
- ✓ Accessible
- ✓ Forty-one rooms

**www.turennemarais.com**

€€-€€€

**Located at 6 Rue de Turenne**
*in the Marais district, 4th arrondissement*
**On the right bank**

**Intl. calling: (011) 33 1 42 78 43 25**
Local calling: 01 42 78 43 25

**Email:** reservation@turennemarais.com

# PART 7

## [All Transport]

**Airport Transfers**
**Le Métro**
**RER Trains**
**Buses**
**& Taxis**

*You have transfer questions and we have the answers*

©L. Osterhoudt

Whether you arrive by air or by train, we have a solution for you to get to your accommodations without a hassle.

Paris' main airport is CDG - Charles de Gaulle International Airport. Getting from the airport to central Paris is easy. Below are some basic tips and prices, but a wealth of information can be found on the airport's own handy website: **http://easycdg.com** -it even has a link for live traffic conditions. Choose your language preference at the top of the page.

*We will not be covering the Paris Orly Airport (ORY) since it is generally used for flights within Europe.*

## Getting from CDG airport to central Paris

**Grab a taxi** from the queue waiting out front of the terminal. (A sign that says TAXI denotes the start of the line.) Depending on traffic, it will take 40 to 50 minutes between the CDG airport and Paris. The price is now a fixed <u>flat</u> rate:

Around €53 between CDG and Paris' right bank
Around €58 between CDG and Paris' left bank

**Take the RER regional train- B Line** which is the least expensive way into the city. It takes less than thirty minutes to get to Paris' *Gare du Nord* train station and continues making many other city-center stops after that. Departs from the Roissypole station near CDG's Terminal 3 about every fifteen minutes but is accessible from all terminals. Cost is around €12.

**Ride a Roissy Bus.** It takes fifty-five minutes to get from the CDG airport to the Paris-Opéra, at 13 Rue Scribe. The service is available outside all three of the airport terminals. Buy a ticket with cash or credit card at any of the departure point machines/booths, or pay in cash on board. Departs from the airport every twenty minutes or so. Cost is around €14 to €17 depending on if you have a Navigo Easy Card to load this special bus ticket on.

# Getting from central Paris, back to CDG airport

**Grab a taxi** from the queue of official Taxi Parisien cars waiting at your local taxi rank. Depending on traffic, it will take 40 to 50 minutes between Paris and the CDG airport. The price is now a fixed <u>flat</u> rate:

Around €53 between Paris' right bank and CDG
Around €58 between Paris' left bank and CDG

**Ride a Roissy Bus** from 13 Rue Scribe, directly across from the famed Palais Garnier Opera House. Departures are from 7:30am to 10:30pm every 20 minutes. Pay the driver in cash onboard, or buy a ticket at any train station or automated ticket machine with cash or a credit card. For information, call locally: 01 49 25 61 87. Cost is around €14 to €17 depending on if you have a Navigo Easy Card to load this special bus ticket on.

**Take the RER regional train– B Line** right to CDG International Airport. (Many city-center Métro stations service the RER B line so it's quite convenient.) The RER B train will whisk you right to the Roissypole station near CDG's terminal 3 and runs about every fifteen minutes or so. The travel time is around thirty minutes and costs around €12.

### *What's our favorite method of transferring?*

We like to do a combo… After a long flight, all we want to do is get to our hotel (even if just to ditch our luggage) so we always splurge on an official taxi upon our arrival at the airport, and then save money by taking the Roissy bus back to the airport at the end of our trip. The Roissy is comfortable and picks up passengers every few minutes right across from the Palais Garnier Opera House. After that it goes non-stop to CDG's terminals. (See *Ride a Roissy Bus*, above)

### *Not flying in?*

If you're arriving in Paris by train from another European country or from a different region in France, find out which of Paris' six train stations you'll be arriving at. This way you'll have some idea of where you are when you get there. All six rail stations connect to the rest of the city by Métro subway, and all have waiting taxi queues.

*Taxis and Uber car are scenic ways to get around Paris and should definitely be budgeted in*

©Alán Duke

# Taxi Clues

**There are fixed taxi rates between Paris and its airports...** to and from the Right Bank is €53; to and from the Left Bank is around €58. An extra fee for luggage handling is normal. A tip is never expected in taxis here.

**Official taxis come in many colors** but all of them will have a sign on top of the vehicle displaying "TAXI PARISEN" that can light up, and a working meter inside showing the cost as you go. If the vehicle's sign is lit then it is available for hire.

For your own safety DO NOT take unlicensed taxis. *Pretending to be an official driver of some type is the easiest way for criminals to prey on unsuspecting tourists.*

**If you call a taxi** (or if your hotel or restaurant calls one for you) its meter will have started running from the moment the car started to come get you.

**Be sure to have cash** as not all Paris taxis accept credit cards. Even when they do, the fare must be above €15 to be allowed on a credit card.

**The general hire is around €7.10** and the cost increments that follow will vary depending if it's after 5pm or on a Sunday. They are between €1.07 per km. and €1,60 per km.

**Paris taxis will stop if you hail them, providing they are available.** If no taxis stop for you, it might be because you're hailing them within a close distance of an official taxi queue.

*The Paris Métro is easy to use but has lots of stairs*

©Richard Soto

# Métro Clues

With its three-hundred stations, Paris has one of the most extensive subway systems in the world. These underground trains run every few minutes from around 5:30am to 12:20am and can get crowded during rush hours. The T+ single tickets and *carnet* packets of ten are being <u>phased out right now</u>. Instead, you'll probably need to purchase a single ride from a ticketing machine (or pay a one-time fee of €2 per person for a reusable pass card called **NavigoEasy**. You must acquire these *from a human inside a métro ticket "service" booth*.

**The new reusable NavigoEasy cards** and can be "loaded" with different rides by that human in the service booth. Once you have it in-hand, you can then load it at one of the regular ticketing machines, or with an app. The popular 10-ride option gives you a discount of sorts.

**Tap your NavigoEasy card on the top area of the turnstile and enter.** Keep it somewhere safe but handy in case you need to show it to officials within the underground system.

**Métro doors do not necessarily open for you automatically.** You may need to push the button on the door to board or to disembark. Locals riding on the Métro like to push the button to open the doors before the train has even stopped which is very exciting indeed.

**On wide escalators, Parisians stand to the right** and walk on the left so be aware of this. Métro maps are free so just ask a ticket agent for one.

**The local buses are not easy to learn** but can be a good way to see the city if you decide to take the time to analyze it. Bus tickets and passes can be purchased in the same manner as the Métro and the RER trains, and are interchangeable when using the new NavigoEasy pass cards.

# RER & Commuter Train Clues

**Paris' Regional Rapid Transit system (RER)** connects the city with the suburbs and is fast because it makes fewer stops than the Métro trains. Its five lines are denoted by letters A B C D and E to differentiate it from the subway trains which are numbered. Some stations within central Paris serve both the Métro and RER.

-*Note that RER regional train fares going outside of central Paris cannot be loaded on that NavigoEasy card.*

**Inserting your RER ticket into the turnstile to open it also validates it.** Do not misplace this ticket as you may be asked to show it upon inspection by train personnel, and **you may also need it to open the turnstile to let you out.** *It automatically includes one free transfer to a Métro subway line.*

**RER's Line C is the one that will take you to Château de Versailles** (or to Orly Airport via connecting lines) should you be going there. **Line B** connects central Paris to terminal 3 at the CDG International Airport.

**The Transilien (*Ter*) commuter train lines travel even further out** and are the trains that will take you to the palace at Fontainebleau.

**The French way to say "round trip"** is *aller-retour* pronounced: *all-lay ray-tour*. Train station associates speak English and all ticket machines do too.

# PART 8

## [Some Final Clues]

**Free Sights**
**Major Museums**
**Festivals and Events**
**Tipping**
**Basic Safety**

# Free Sights

Arc de Triomphe exterior
Basilica Sacré-Cœur Church
Canal Saint-Martin neighborhood
Champs-Elysée Boulevard
Jardin de Luxembourg
Madeleine Church, and many others
Marais neighborhood shopping
Montmartre hilltop area
Musée Carnevalet – History of Paris Museum
Musée Cognacq-Jay – 18th century Exhibits Museum
Notre Dame Cathedral - *exterior only at present*
Rue Mouffetard
Saint-Germain-de-Prés Church
Victor Hugo's Apartment

# Main Museums

Centre Pompidou*
Cluny Middle Ages Museum*
Decorative Arts Museum
French Army Museum*
Gustave Moreau Museum*
Hôtel de la Marine
Louvre Museum*
Montmartre Museum
National Museum of Modern Art
National Museum of Natural History
Orangerie Museum*
Orsay Museum*
Picasso Museum
Rodin Museum*
Sewer Museum*

*Reviewed in this book*

# Main Festivals and Events

### Le Tour de France & Bastille Day

Paris has two major summertime celebrations: the final lap of the famed *Tour de France* cycling race on the last Sunday of July, and the French Independence Day (called Bastille Day) which is always held on July 14th. These two celebrations will increase the number of people visiting Paris and will also impact the availability of restaurant tables and hotel rooms, not to mention the prices of the latter. That said, major events can also provide visitors with an unforgettable experience.

Visitors to Paris should also be aware of the May 1 (Labor Day) holiday as well, when many businesses and even major sights are often closed.

The truth is that Paris has so many things going on year round, from the *Festival Paris Cinéma* to the Paris International Marathon (and everything in between) that it's best to view an *events* calendar for the month you're planning to go. You'll find some very helpful information at the official website below:

**http://en.parisinfo.com**

# Tipping Clues

Unlike some guide books, websites, and articles touting so-called travel advice, we're going to be completely honest here and go against all that useful information regarding tipping in Paris. Why? *Because we have French friends who live in Paris.* Many of them. And they all agree on one thing: only unwitting Americans tip in Paris. This is their advice...

**Dining:** In a café: Zero tip. / In a fine restaurant: Zero tip. (See note below!)

**Taxis:** Zero tip

**Shuttle Bus driver:** Zero tip

**Hôtel concierge**: €5 to €20 if they got you tickets that were impossible to find.

**Hôtel room housekeeper:** Zero tip

**Bellman:** €2 if he brings all your baggage to your room.

**Bathroom attendants:** €1 or less, unless there's a sign stating an expected amount

**Coat checks:** Zero tip

**Hair stylist:** Zero tip

**Tour guides:** Zero tip (Some companies post a sign that tips are not accepted)

**Seine Boat Hosts:** Tip at your discretion if you enjoyed their banter.

**Theatre ushers:** Zero tip (By the way, the printed program is not free)

In restaurants, never ask if the tip or service is included because they will always say no (thinking that you're referring to an *extra* gratuity.)

Here are the facts: a 15% service charge will *always* be added to your dining bill –it's the law. The words *service compris* (service included) printed on your check (or just on the menu card) may not be obvious, but the amount will be in your total. Trust us.

*But if you simply must leave a tip because it's a very fine restaurant and you just had the best waiter of your life and you might even invite him or her to stay at your house when they come to the States, here are the guidelines:* **While you may round up a few euros on a credit card, never leave coin on the table. It is considered very rude. Give paper currency if you must; 6% ought to suffice.**

# Money Clues

**Some banks and credit card companies** still appreciate a phone call to let them know you'll be traveling abroad. Call them just in case to avoid any hassles in Europe.

**American debit cards work just fine at France's ATM machines** but in Paris you may not be able to avoid incurring a fee for each withdrawal; don't go to an ATM more than you have to. (This fee is applied to most debit and credit cards, even debit cards who tout their 'no overseas fees' policy – they mean no fees at *their* end, and have no control over what other banks may charge.)

**Calculate the amount of your personal daily withdrawal limit** *in euros* so that you don't think your bank card has been rejected in France when it's actually because you merely tried to take out too much at once or on the same day.

**Use your debit card for purchases wisely.** Since there may be a fee with each use, you might not want to debit that €3 gelato. The fee may be more than the cone! Try to find a travel-friendly fee-free credit card before your trip. This is where the CapOne debit card really shines; as long as you choose the Euro button and *not* the US Currency button when doing the transaction, there will be no added fees at all.

**For the best exchange rate, get your cash out of an ATM that is located at or owned by an actual bank,** such as BNP Paribas, rather than one that is operated by a private money "exchange" company; their ATM machines look just like the bank's in order to deceive you, so go by the name that's advertised on it. Definitely be aware of the ones called "Euronet" because their rates are downright criminal.

**If you exchange your travel money into euro currency** *before* **leaving home,** you will (1) have to guess at the amount you'll be spending, (2) be charged a much high exchange rate and fee, and (3) be charged that high exchange rate a *second time* when you exchange your leftover cash back to your home currency after the trip. Don't do it. Use the ATMs at Paris banks and withdraw an amount of money that can last you a few days. It doesn't hurt to take a small amount of euros along with you though; we always bring €50 to have on hand for incidentals upon arrival.

**Spend all of your euro coins** by the end of your visit because they're not exchangeable.

**In Paris, hotels and rental properties will usually charge a small room tax** of around €1 to €5 per person, per night. This is customarily paid in cash directly to the hotel when you check-out, so be ready for it or ask in advance.

**You may be eligible for a VAT partial-tax refund on certain purchases.** Always take your passport with you if you plan to do any major shopping; it will be required in order to request a tax refund. Ask the sales associate to file the digital application (if available) right to your credit or debit card so that your refund is automatic. This way you won't have to do anything at the airport and can proceed right to your departure gate. *Note: You will not receive a VAT refund for any items that you ship home.*

# Telephone Clues

**Know how to make a telephone call to and from Paris:**

**From the US or Canada, to Paris**
Dial 011 then 33 (France) and then the phone number *without any zero* preceding it.

If the number is 05 84 84 84 97, you would dial:
(011) 33 5 84 84 84 97.


**From Paris, to the US or Canada**
Dial 001 then the area code, plus the seven digit phone number. If you hear a recording in French just wait a moment; the ringing will start after it.


**From the United Kingdom to Paris**
Dial 0033 and then French phone number *minus the leading zero.*

If the number is 05 84 84 84 97 you would dial:
(0033) 5 84 84 84 97


**From Paris to the United Kingdom**
Dial 0044 and then British phone number.

If the number is 20 7323-8299 you would dial:
(0044) 20 7323-8299


**From within Paris, to Paris**
Dial the entire ten digit phone number, leaving in the leading zero, like:
05 84 84 84 97
*-No country code (33) or other numbers are needed.*

*Are you thinking,*
"Hey, when calling from the US to Italy you never leave out a zero."

*We reply,*
"This ain't Italy. Leave the zero out when dialing internationally to France."

*-Details in our books, Clued In Venice, Clued In Rome, and Clued In Florence.*

*Marie-Antoinette had a fake village hamlet built near her Petit Trianon mansion*

©Richard Soto

# Your Embassy

If for any reason you feel you need to reach out to your embassy, (passport problems, safety, legal problems, etc.) here is the necessary information:

*American Embassy in Paris:*
Local Paris call: 01 43 12 22 22
Overseas call: (011) 33 1 43 12 22 22
-Located at 2 Avenue Gabriel, 75008 Paris

*Canadian Embassy in Paris:*
Local Paris call: 01 44 43 29 02
Overseas call: (011) 33 1 44 43 29 02
-Located at 130 Rue du Faubourg Saint-Honoré, 75008 Paris

*British Embassy in Paris:*
Local Paris call: 01 44 51 31 00
From the UK call: (0033) 1 44 51 31 00
-Located at 35 Rue du Faubourg Saint-Honoré, 75008 Paris

## Safety and Common Sense

Paris is obviously not a crime free city; it is a real city, with a complex society and a complex people. But that doesn't mean you'll feel unsafe here. Quite the contrary, especially when referring to the city center. Still, a bit of caution can go a long way so protect your valuables the same way you would anywhere, by using the electronic safe in your hotel room and by keeping money tucked out of sight. And never leave your new luggage unattended out front of your hotel. Like any place with crowds and foreigners, there can be an increased chance of being pick-pocketed especially in the Métro system or in a crowded museum. Ladies: close and fasten your handbag. Men: keep your wallet anywhere except your back pocket.

Paris' public and very modern self-cleaning toilettes are usually free (or a nominal fee) and can be found throughout the city.

Bottles, bottles, everywhere. Should you help out the environment by foregoing the plastic and asking your waiter for tap water instead? *Oui, mais bien sûr!* Paris has clean, excellent tasting drinking water and it's free in any restaurant or café. You can ask for it by the glass or carafe, without any worry of stomach ills. Even the many public drinking fountains are safe to use and a few of the newer ones even offer bubbly, sparkling, fizzy water! Only in Paris.

# Emergency?  Dial 17

In general, if you ever feel unwell here, there are pharmacies all over Paris. Look for *Pharmacie* signs indicated with the symbol of a green cross. Your hotel can call a medical professional for you if required, another good reason to stay at a full service hotel.

Europe has a different electrical current than the U.S., and to make matters more difficult, the plug style (and shape) that allows you to connect to an electrical outlet is even different between Paris and Great Britain. This means you need to be prepared. Take a couple of plug adaptors with you, the more the better. Don't worry, they're cheap and can be ordered on amazon.com which is much easier than running all over town trying to find them. Plan in advance!

We don't recommend taking *electrical converters* with you because we don't trust them. They rarely work on things like blow dryers, even though the companies making them claim that they will convert the electrical current on any appliance. Most decent hotels supply a blow dryer for you because it's cheaper than paying to repair that burned room.

As for your iPhone, laptop, or other high-tech toy... they're already made dual-voltage so the only thing you need to worry about is getting that plug adapter so you can actually plug it in!

# From the Authors

We've had so much fun bringing this book to you and sincerely hope you found it useful. The star rating offered to you at the end is for metadata use only and does not affect our online stars. If you enjoyed *Clued In Paris*, please take a moment to leave a short customer review on Amazon.com so that your rating will count for us. Even a few sentences would be greatly appreciated.

Our blog is easily accessible and offers additional information to travelers between our annual updates. We also field any and all questions, comments, advice, and suggestions at <u>cluedintravelbooks@gmail.com</u>.

If you're looking for experiences that will take your Parisian visit to the next level, check out our super fun *Bored in Paris*, now in ebook and print at: **www.amazon.com/dp/B09N58397Q**

Thank you so much for your support. Check out our other cool Clued In travel books, all exclusively on Amazon.

*Clued In Venice*
*Clued In Rome*
*Clued In Florence*
*Clued In Barcelona*
*Clued In London*
*Clued In Edinburgh*
*Clued In Miami*
*Clued In New York*
*Clued In San Francisco*

**For more information on this or other ©Clued In travel spots, visit our city-by-city blog at www.cluedintravelbooks.com**

# Disclaimer

Every effort has been made for accuracy. All weblinks and URL's herein were accurate and live at the time of publishing, but travel information is fluid and prone to change. The authors, publishers, and webmasters take no responsibility for consequences or mishaps while using this book, nor are they responsible for any difficulties, inconveniences, injuries, illness, medical mishaps, or other physical issues related to the information and suggestions provided in this book. The information contained in this book is for diversionary purposes only. Any mentions in this book do not represent an endorsement of any group or company or their practices, methods, or any mishaps that may occur when hired or participated in.

In no event will we be liable for any loss or damage including without limitation, indirect or consequential loss or damage, or any loss or damage whatsoever arising from loss of data or profits arising out of, or in connection with, the use of this eBook.

Through this eBook you're able to link to other websites which are not under the control of *Clued In Travel Books* or its authors or associates. We have no control over the nature, content and availability of those sites. The inclusion of any links does not necessarily imply a recommendation or endorse the views expressed within them.

Every effort is made to provide live links that are up to date and working properly. However, *Clued In Travel Books* or its authors or associates take no responsibility for, and will not be liable for, the links or associated websites being temporarily unavailable due to technical issues beyond our control, or any mishaps occurring from such issues.

# My notes

# My notes

# My notes